Praying with Saint Paul

USING *LECTIO DIVINA*

Acts of the Apostles

NEW AMERICAN BIBLE

FOR INDIVIDUAL AND COMMUNITY PRAYER

Library of Congress Control Number: 2009922037

Revised New Testament
Nihil Obstat: Stephen J. Hartdegen, O.F.M., S.S.L.
                     Censor Deputatus

Imprimatur: + James A. Hickey, S.T.D., J.C.D.
                     Archbishop of Washington
August 27, 1986

***Lectio Divina* Text**
Nihil Obstat: Reverend Lawrence Frizzell, D.Phil.
                     Censor Librorum

Imprimatur: + Most Rev. John J. Myers, DD., J.C.D.
                     Archbishop of Newark
July 11, 2008

The Nihil Obstat and Imprimatur are official declarations that the material reviewed is free of doctrinal or moral error. No implication is contained therein that those granting the Nihil Obstat and Imprimatur agree with the contents, opinions, or statements expressed.

ISBN: 978-0-8091-4645-1

Published by Paulist Press
997 Macarthur Boulevard
Mahwah, New Jersey, 07430

www.paulistpress.com

Printed and bound in China.

APC-FT7227

INTRODUCTION

Lawrence Boadt, CSP

Saint Paul gives us our most important window into the preaching of the apostles and the beliefs of the earliest Christians. He was converted soon after Jesus' Resurrection, was active for thirty years as an apostle, wrote at least ten letters to the first churches, and died before a single Gospel as we now know them was written. We have more details about his life during those years than of anyone else in the New Testament, and yet, for most people, Paul remains a shadowy and mysterious figure. In addition, we read from his letters on well over half of the Sundays of the year, and yet have a hard time getting a sense of Paul as a whole person and of his thought. Part of this is due to the organization of our Lectionary of Scripture Readings for Sundays, in which the reading from Paul's letters is sandwiched between an Old Testament text and a Gospel passage. As a result, homilists rarely preach on Paul. This is a great loss to our faith and spirituality. For not only is Paul the first of all Christian proclaimers of the Gospel of Jesus Christ, but he is still the most fundamental and profound of spiritual thinkers about the mystery of Christ.

There are thirteen letters in the New Testament said to actually be written by Paul himself. Yet if three or four of them were set down by his disciples in his name, they all breathe the living spirit and personality of the man. To really understand the power of the Gospel, one must read Paul's own words in which his energetic and vivid passion for what God has done in Jesus shines forth.

In addition to Paul's own letters, we are lucky to also have a detailed account of Paul's ministry from St. Luke, who wrote both the Gospel of Luke and the Acts of the Apostles. The Acts is a marvelous work, detailing how the Good News was brought from Jerusalem to Rome itself, as Jesus had commanded at his Ascension, and how it won over both Jews and pagans alike. The early chapters of Acts tell the story of Peter guiding the spread of the Gospel in Jerusalem and the surrounding areas of Judea and Samaria. Then in chapter 9, it begins to turn its attention to Paul, the apostle to the pagan nations and a tireless missionary who would travel through the entire Mediterranean world.

Luke notes the beginnings of Paul's life as a missionary in small sections of chapters 9, 11, and 12, while concluding the stories about Peter. Beginning in chapter 13, however, the narrative turns entirely to Paul, all the way to the end in chapter 28. The narrative follows Paul from his work in Antioch up to his imprisonment in Rome around 60 A.D. Paul was released and continued to preach for several more years before being executed by Nero between 64 and 67 A.D. As told in Acts, Paul's life is an adventure story, but it is also an inspiring example of an apostle who fully lived the Gospel he preached.

One can read Paul's story in Acts as a way to trace the history of the early church, but Luke intended it to show us how the Holy Spirit guides the growth of faith in every different sort of person, and how the Spirit sustains the courage and perseverance of those who really hear and embrace the Gospel message through all the difficulties and persecutions we are forced to endure. It is an inspiring story, and no one in this story inspires as deeply and richly as Paul himself. That is why this small book of the Acts of the Apostles, with reflections for *Lectio Divina* reading and prayer, is offered as a helpful way to begin to know Paul more fully as a spiritual source for ourselves and, through him, to discover the presence and power of Christ and the Holy Spirit in our own daily lives.

To help make reading Acts a little easier, the following chronology of Paul's life is offered. All dates are approximate and many are only suggestions based on scholarly guesswork. The only certain date is the appearance of Paul before the proconsul Gallio in Corinth, which is reported in Acts 18:12–17. From an inscription at Delphi, we know that Gallio's term of office lasted only one year, from 51 to 52 A.D. Other dates for Paul are usually calculated backward and forward from this point.

Event	A.D.
Paul's birth	6 to10
Jesus' death and resurrection	30
The stoning of Stephen	32 to 33
Paul's conversion	33 or 34
His time in Arabia (Gal 1:17; 2Cor 11:32)	35 to 38
His time in Tarsus	38 to 43 or 44
Ministry in Antioch	43 to 45
First missionary journey	45 to 48
Council of Jerusalem	48
Second missionary journey	49 to 52
First Letter to the Thessalonians	50
Second Letter to the Thessalonians	51
Paul's time in Corinth	51 to 52
Third Missionary Journey	53 to 56
Letter to the Galatians	53
Time in Ephesus	53 and 56
Letter to the Philippians	55
First Letter to the Corinthians	55
Letter to Philemon	56
Letter to the Romans	56
Second Letter to the Corinthians	56
Paul's return to Jerusalem	56 or 57
Prison in Caesarea	56 to 58
Journey to Rome	59
Roman imprisonment	60 to 61
Release? Journey to Spain?	61 to 63 to 66
Further imprisonment and death	63 to 67

The last period of Paul's life is very uncertain. If Paul was released after the two years stay in Rome, as Acts 28 implies, then he may have had as many as five years of further ministry in both the areas of Asia and Greece that he had traveled so often, and also possibly a visit to Spain. It would have been in this period that he composed the Letters to the Colossians and to the Ephesians, and the Pastoral Letters to Timothy and Titus. Many scholars believe, however, that these were written in Paul's name by his disciples after his death.

HOW TO USE THE CATHOLIC PRAYER BIBLE WITH *LECTIO DIVINA*

Lawrence Boadt, CSP

Reflective reading of Scripture as a way to lead us into prayer has been a practice in the Church from the earliest centuries. It can take many forms, from singing the psalms as a community, to reciting the Our Father, to reading each section of a biblical book systematically with pauses for reflection and prayer. This last method is often called *Lectio Divina*, from the Latin for "divine reading." Spiritual writers describe *Lectio Divina* in a variety of ways, but all agree that divine reading has a definite pattern. That pattern is described here briefly in four steps, which are done in order:

A slow and thoughtful reading of a passage from the Bible
A time of reflection and thinking about the meaning of that text to me as a reader
A period of prayer to God to bring the message or wisdom of the text to fruit in myself
A decision on what I should do as a result; that is, an action plan to change or improve my life

Lectio Divina is simple enough to be done any place where there is some quiet or peace, and at any time of day when you can find a few minutes. It can last for as long or short as you wish to make it; you can spend three minutes or fifteen. And it is intended for everyone, for you—not just for those people you may think of as elite in some way: priests and religious, the very educated, or the very pious. Everyone—including you as you are right now—can find pleasure and spiritual enrichment in *Lectio Divina*. The only real requirement is to concentrate on what you are doing through each of the four steps so that you are not distracted and forget where you are at. If you do become distracted, don't give up. Just bring your thoughts back to the text. What's important is to hold the four steps together so that the reading actually turns to prayer.

In this book, there is a suggested four-step meditation for each chapter of the Acts of the Apostles (and sometimes two per chapter!). Because there are twenty-eight chapters in Acts, this allows you to use this book to discover or practice *Lectio Divina* once a day for a month, or each day of the Lenten season, or twice a day for two weeks. How often is not the most important decision you make. The commitment to continue it to the end of Acts is. For part of the spiritual richness of the Acts of the Apostles is that, by reflecting on the whole book, you will come to know the traditions of Peter and Paul as people of faith more profoundly, and to better pray with them and through their example.

Here are the four steps we suggest for every meditation; however, remember that these four steps are not the only way you can reflect on that passage. They are just a way for you to start.

1. Read. The first step gives you a very brief description of what the biblical passage meant when it was written, but clearly there is more to be found in the text than this very short thought. This one insight invites the reader to seek others.

2. Reflect. The second step draws out some implication from the situation described in the reading, but again there are certainly many more you might see and meditate on.

3. Pray. This next step suggests only one or two possible ways to begin a prayer. Hopefully, the reader will add many more, and literally pray up a storm!

4. Act. The final step in *Lectio Divina* is typically a resolution, and each person will surely have their own that applies to their own life.

As a whole, the meditations are intended to stimulate us to discover our own way of praying and our own way of speaking with God, especially when the ordinary words of fixed prayers are no longer enough.

This is an introduction to what should hopefully become a lifelong source of fulfilling prayer. After all, what better way to converse with God than sharing together the very words that our divine Friend Himself inspired, so that we would know Him and come to Him for our salvation.

This book is taken from the forthcoming *Catholic Prayer Bible*. For further information, see the advertisement on the inside back cover.

Acts of the Apostles

THE ACTS OF THE APOSTLES, the second volume of Luke's two-volume work, continues Luke's presentation of biblical history, describing how the salvation promised to Israel in the Old Testament and accomplished by Jesus has now under the guidance of the holy Spirit been extended to the Gentiles. This was accomplished through the divinely chosen representatives (Acts 10:41) whom Jesus prepared during his historical ministry (Acts 1:21–22) and commissioned after his resurrection as witnesses to all that he taught (Acts 1:8; 10:37–43; Lk 24:48). Luke's preoccupation with the Christian community as the Spirit-guided bearer of the word of salvation rules out of his book detailed histories of the activity of most of the preachers. Only the main lines of the roles of Peter and Paul serve Luke's interest.

Peter was the leading member of the Twelve (Acts 1:13, 15), a miracle worker like Jesus in the gospel (Acts 3:1–10; 5:1–11, 15; 9:32–35, 36–42), the object of divine care (Acts 5:17–21; 12:6–11), and the spokesman for the Christian community (Acts 2:14–36; 3:12–26; 4:8–12; 5:29–32; 10:34–43; 15:7–11), who, according to Luke, was largely responsible for the growth of the community in the early days (Acts 2:4; 4:4). Paul eventually joined the community at Antioch (Acts 11:25–26), which subsequently commissioned him and Barnabas to undertake the spread of the gospel to Asia Minor. This missionary venture generally failed to win the Jews of the diaspora to the gospel but enjoyed success among the Gentiles (Acts 13:14—14:27).

Paul's refusal to impose the Mosaic law upon his Gentile converts provoked very strong objection among the Jewish Christians of Jerusalem (Acts 15:1), but both Peter and James supported his position (Acts 15:6–21). Paul's second and third mission-ary journeys (Acts 16:36—21:16) resulted in the same pattern of failure among the Jews gen-erally but of some success among the Gentiles. Paul, like Peter, is presented as a miracle worker (Acts 14:8–18; 19:12; 20:7–12; 28:7–10) and the object of divine care (Acts 16:25–31).

In Acts, Luke has provided a broad survey of the church's development from the resur-rection of Jesus to Paul's first Roman imprisonment, the point at which the book ends. In telling this story, Luke describes the emergence of Christianity from its origins in Judaism to its position as a religion of worldwide status and appeal. Originally a Jewish Christian communi-ty in Jerusalem, the church was placed in circumstances impelling it to include within its mem-bership people of other cultures: the Samaritans (Acts 8:4–25), at first an occasional Gentile (Acts 8:26–30; 10:1–48), and finally the Gentiles on principle (Acts 11:20–21). Fear on the part of the Jewish people that Christianity, particularly as preached to the Gentiles, threatened their own cultural heritage caused them to be suspicious of Paul's gospel (Acts 13:42–45; 15:1–5; 28:17–24). The inability of Christian missionaries to allay this apprehension inevitably created a situation in which the gospel was preached more and more to the Gentiles. Toward the end of Paul's career, the Christian communities, with the exception of those in Palestine itself (Acts 9:31), were mainly of Gentile membership. In tracing the emergence of Christian-ity from Judaism, Luke is insistent upon the prominence of Israel in the divine plan of salva-tion (see the note on Acts 1:26; see also Acts 2:5–6; 3:13–15; 10:36; 13:16–41; 24:14–15) and that the extension of salvation to the Gentiles has been a part of the divine plan from the beginning (see Acts 15:13–18; 26:22–23).

In the development of the church from a Jewish Christian origin in Jerusalem, with its roots in Jewish religious tradition, to a series of Christian communities among the Gentiles of the Roman empire, Luke perceives the action of God in history laying open the heart of all hu-manity to the divine message of salvation. His approach to the history of the church is moti-vated by his theological interests. His history of the apostolic church is the story of a Spirit-guided community and a Spirit-guided spread of the Word of God (Acts 1:8). The trav-els of Peter and Paul are in reality the travels of the Word of God as it spreads from Jerusalem, the city of destiny for Jesus, to Rome, the capital of the civilized world of Luke's day. Nonethe-less, the historical data he utilizes are of value for the understanding of the church's early life and development and as general background to the Pauline epistles. In the interpretation of Acts, care must be exercised to determine Luke's theological aims and interests and to evalu-ate his historical data without either exaggerating their literal accuracy or underestimating their factual worth.

Finally, an apologetic concern is evident throughout Acts. By stressing the continuity be-tween Judaism and Christianity (Acts 13:16–41; 23:6–9; 24:10–21; 26:2–23), Luke argues that Christianity is deserving of the same toleration accorded Judaism by Rome. Part of Paul's de-fense before Roman authorities is to show that Christianity is not a disturber of the peace of the Roman Empire (Acts 24:5, 12–13; 25:7–8). Moreover, when he stands before Roman author-ities, he is declared innocent of any crime against the empire (Acts 18:13–15; 23:29; 25:25–27; 26:31–32). Luke tells his story with the hope that Christianity will be treated as fairly.

Concerning the date of Acts, see the Introduction to the Gospel according to Luke.

The principal divisions of the Acts of the Apostles are the following:

   I. The Preparation for the Christian Mission (1:1—2:13)
   II. The Mission in Jerusalem (2:14—8:3)
   III. The Mission in Judea and Samaria (8:4—9:43)
   IV. The Inauguration of the Gentile Mission (10:1—15:35)
   V. The Mission of Paul to the Ends of the Earth (15:36—28:31)

Read Acts 1:1–11

Acts is a second volume, a continuation written by the author of the Gospel of Luke. The intended recipient is "Theophilus," a name based on two Greek words, theos (God) and philos (love). For forty days, Jesus appeared to his followers before ascending to heaven. The mission of proclaiming the gospel continues after Jesus' ascension.

Reflect: The two men dressed in white garments ask: "Why are you standing there looking at the sky?" Where is my gaze directed?

Pray: Jesus reassures his followers. They are not to be preoccupied or worried about the future. Pray for the willingness to deal with future uncertainties, so that you can use your time well as we await the Lord's return in glory.

Act: Am I a person who "loves God" as I read and reflect on the words of sacred scripture? Do I see each day as an opportunity to continue making the gospel message known?

The Promise of the Spirit.

1 [1*a] In the first book, Theophilus, I dealt with all that Jesus did and taught [2b] until the day he was taken up, after giving instructions through the holy Spirit to the apostles whom he had chosen. [3c] He presented himself alive to them by many proofs after he had suffered, appearing to them during forty days* and speaking about the kingdom of God. [4d] While meeting with them, he enjoined them not to depart from Jerusalem, but to wait for "the promise of the Father* about which you have heard me speak; [5e] for John baptized with water, but in a few days you will be baptized with the holy Spirit."

The Ascension of Jesus.

[6] When they had gathered together they asked him, "Lord, are you at this time going* to restore the kingdom to Israel?" [7*f] He answered them, "It is not for you to know the times or seasons that the Father has established by his own authority. [8*g] But you will receive power when the holy Spirit comes upon you, and you will be my witnesses in Jerusalem, throughout Judea and Samaria, and to the ends of the earth." [9h] When he had said this, as they were looking on, he was lifted up, and a cloud took him from their sight. [10i] While they were looking intently at the sky as he was going, suddenly two men dressed in white garments stood beside them. [11j] They said, "Men of Galilee, why are you standing there looking at the sky? This Jesus who has been taken up from you into heaven will return in the same way as you have seen him going into heaven." [12k] Then they returned to Jerusalem from the mount called Olivet, which is near Jerusalem, a sabbath day's journey away.

The First Community in Jerusalem.

[13] When they entered the city they went to the upper room where they were staying, Peter and John and James and Andrew, Philip and Thomas, Bartholomew and Matthew, James son of Alphaeus, Simon the Zealot, and Judas son of James. [14l] All these devoted themselves with one accord to prayer, together with some women, and Mary the mother of Jesus, and his brothers.

The Choice of Judas's Successor.

[15] During those days Peter stood up in the midst of the brothers (there was a group of about one hundred

a. [1:1] Lk 1:1–4.
b. [1:2] Mt 28:19–20; Lk 24:44–49; Jn 20:22; 1Tm 3:16.
c. [1:3] 10:41; 13:31.
d. [1:4] Jn 14:16, 17, 26.
e. [1:5] 11:16; Mt 3:11; Mk 1:8; Lk 3:16; Jn 1:26; Eph 1:13.
f. [1:7] Mt 24:36; 1Thes 5:1–2.
g. [1:8] 2:1–13; 10:39; Is 43:10; Mt 28:19; Lk 24:47–48.
h. [1:9] 2Kgs 2:11; Mk 16:19; Lk 24:51.
i. [1:10] Jn 20:17.
j. [1:11] Lk 24:51; Eph 4:8–10; 1 Pt 3:22; Rev 1:7.
k. [1:12–14] Lk 6:14–16.
l. [1:14] Lk 23:49.

Read Acts 1:12–26

After careful consideration, prayer, and the casting of lots, Matthias is chosen to replace Judas.

Reflect: Reflect on the meaning of the verse, "May another take his office," derived from Psalm 109:8.

Pray: Important decisions and the process of discernment need to include prayer. Seek God's guidance and reflect prayerfully when you are facing big decisions in your life.

Act: In what ways do I see myself as having been chosen to continue the mission of the apostles?

Read Acts 2:1–13

The promised Holy Spirit descends upon the disciples in a dramatic way during the feast of Pentecost. Bold deeds result.

Reflect: What is the significance of this Pentecost event?

Pray: God's mighty acts are to be proclaimed. Seek the Holy Spirit's guidance in your daily life.

Act: Be grateful for what God has done for you in your life. Share this sense of gratitude with others.

and twenty persons in the one place). He said, 16m "My brothers, the scripture had to be fulfilled which the holy Spirit spoke beforehand through the mouth of David, concerning Judas, who was the guide for those who arrested Jesus. 17 He was numbered among us and was allotted a share in this ministry. 18n He bought a parcel of land with the wages of his iniquity, and falling headlong, he burst open in the middle, and all his insides spilled out.* 19 This became known to everyone who lived in Jerusalem, so that the parcel of land was called in their language 'Akeldama,' that is, Field of Blood. 20o For it is written in the Book of Psalms:

'Let his encampment become desolate,
    and may no one dwell in it.'

And:

'May another take his office.'

21 Therefore, it is necessary that one of the men who accompanied us the whole time the Lord Jesus came and went among us, 22p beginning from the baptism of John until the day on which he was taken up from us, become with us a witness to his resurrection."

23 So they proposed two, Joseph called Barsabbas, who was also known as Justus, and Matthias. 24 Then they prayed, "You, Lord, who know the hearts of all, show which one of these two you have chosen 25 to take the place in this apostolic ministry from which Judas turned away to go to his own place." 26*q Then they gave lots to them, and the lot fell upon Matthias, and he was counted with the eleven apostles.

The Coming of the Spirit.

2 1*a When the time for Pentecost was fulfilled, they were all in one place together. 2b And suddenly there came from the sky a noise like a strong driving wind,* and it filled the entire house in which they were. 3c Then there appeared to them tongues as of fire,* which parted and came to rest on each one of them. 4d And they were all filled with the holy Spirit and began to speak in different tongues,* as the Spirit enabled them to proclaim.

5 Now there were devout Jews from every nation under heaven staying in Jerusalem. 6 At this sound, they gathered in a large crowd, but they were confused because each one heard them speaking in his own language. 7e They were astounded, and in amazement they asked, "Are not all these people who are speaking Galileans? 8 Then how does each of us hear them in his own native language? 9 We are Parthians, Medes, and

m. [1:16] Ps 41:10; Lk 22:47.
n. [1:18] Mt 27:3–10.
o. [1:20] Ps 69:26; 109:8; Jn 17:12.
p. [1:22] 1:8–9; 10:39.
q. [1:26] Prv 16:33

a. [2:1] Lv 23:15–21; Dt 16:9–11.
b. [2:2–3] Jn 3:8.
c. [2:3] Lk 3:16.
d. [2:4] 1:5; 4:31; 8:15, 17; 10:44;
    11:15–16; 15:8; 19:6; Ps 104:30;
    Jn 20:33.
e. [2:7] 1:11.

Elamites, inhabitants of Mesopotamia, Judea and Cappadocia, Pontus and Asia, 10 Phrygia and Pamphylia, Egypt and the districts of Libya near Cyrene, as well as travelers from Rome, 11f both Jews and converts to Judaism, Cretans and Arabs, yet we hear them speaking in our own tongues of the mighty acts of God." 12 They were all astounded and bewildered, and said to one another, "What does this mean?" 13g But others said, scoffing, "They have had too much new wine."

II: THE MISSION IN JERUSALEM

Read Acts 2:14–41

Peter delivers a speech in which the Pentecost event is explained as the fulfillment of the prophecy of Joel. Convincing proof that Jesus is indeed the messiah results in the conversion of about three thousand people.

Reflect: What does it mean to accept Jesus as the messiah?

Pray: Many are still seeking the messiah. Pray that the Spirit may direct them in their search.

Act: How do I heed the message that I must save myself "from this corrupt generation"?

Peter's Speech at Pentecost.

14* Then Peter stood up with the Eleven, raised his voice, and proclaimed to them, "You who are Jews, indeed all of you staying in Jerusalem. Let this be known to you, and listen to my words. 15 These people are not drunk, as you suppose, for it is only nine o'clock in the morning. 16 No, this is what was spoken through the prophet Joel:

17h 'It will come to pass in the last days,' God says,
    'that I will pour out a portion of my spirit upon all flesh.
Your sons and your daughters shall prophesy,
    your young men shall see visions,
    your old men shall dream dreams.
18 Indeed, upon my servants and my handmaids
    I will pour out a portion of my spirit in those days,
    and they shall prophesy.
19 And I will work wonders in the heavens above
    and signs on the earth below:
    blood, fire, and a cloud of smoke.
20 The sun shall be turned to darkness,
    and the moon to blood,
    before the coming of the great and splendid day of the Lord,
21i and it shall be that everyone shall be saved who calls on
    the name of the Lord.'

22j You who are Israelites, hear these words. Jesus the Nazorean was a man commended to you by God with mighty deeds, wonders, and signs, which God worked through him in your midst, as you yourselves know. 23k This man, delivered up by the set plan and foreknowledge of God, you killed, using lawless men to crucify him. 24l But God raised him up, releasing him from the throes of death, because it was impossible for him to be held by it. 25m For David says of him:

'I saw the Lord ever before me,
    with him at my right hand I shall not be disturbed.

f. [2:11] 10:46.
g. [2:13] 1Cor 14:23.
h. [2:17] Is 2:2; 44:3; Jl 3:1–5.
i. [2:21] Rom 10:13.
j. [2:22] 10:38; Lk 24:19.
k. [2:23] 1Thes 2:15.
l. [2:24] 13:34.
m. [2:25–28] Ps 16:8–11.

Read Acts 2:42–47

The portrayal of Christian communal life is summarized and presented as an ideal.

Reflect: What are the key aspects in this depiction of community?

Pray: Communal life offers great opportunities as well as many challenges. Pray for the grace to deal effectively with some aspect of your community life that needs improvement.

Act: Perform some charitable act as a way of demonstrating that your faith is more than a matter of mere words.

[26] Therefore my heart has been glad and my tongue has exulted;
my flesh, too, will dwell in hope,
[27n] because you will not abandon my soul to the netherworld,
nor will you suffer your holy one to see corruption.
[28] You have made known to me the paths of life;
you will fill me with joy in your presence.'

[29] My brothers, one can confidently say to you about the patriarch David that he died and was buried, and his tomb is in our midst to this day. [30o] But since he was a prophet and knew that God had sworn an oath to him that he would set one of his descendants upon his throne, [31p] he foresaw and spoke of the resurrection of the Messiah, that neither was he abandoned to the netherworld nor did his flesh see corruption. [32] God raised this Jesus; of this we are all witnesses. [33q] Exalted at the right hand of God,* he received the promise of the holy Spirit from the Father and poured it forth, as you [both] see and hear. [34r] For David did not go up into heaven, but he himself said:

'The Lord said to my Lord, "Sit at my right hand
[35] until I make your enemies your footstool."'

[36s] Therefore let the whole house of Israel know for certain that God has made him both Lord and Messiah, this Jesus whom you crucified."

[37t] Now when they heard this, they were cut to the heart, and they asked Peter and the other apostles, "What are we to do, my brothers?" [38u] Peter [said] to them, "Repent and be baptized,* every one of you, in the name of Jesus Christ for the forgiveness of your sins; and you will receive the gift of the holy Spirit. [39v] For the promise is made to you and to your children and to all those far off, whomever the Lord our God will call." [40w] He testified with many other arguments, and was exhorting them, "Save yourselves from this corrupt generation." [41x] Those who accepted his message were baptized, and about three thousand persons were added that day.

Communal Life.

[42*y] They devoted themselves to the teaching of the apostles and to the communal life, to the breaking of the bread and to the prayers.[z] [43a] Awe came upon everyone, and many wonders and signs were done through the apostles. [44b] All who believed were together and had all things in common; [45] they would sell their property and possessions and divide them among all according to each one's need. [46] Every day they devoted themselves to meeting together in the temple area

n. [2:27] 13:35.
o. [2:30] 2Sm 7:12; Ps 132:11.
p. [2:31] 13:35; Ps 16:10.
q. [2:33] 1:4–5.
r. [2:34–35] Ps 110:1.
s. [2:36] 9:22; Rom 10:9; Phil 2:11.
t. [2:37] Lk 3:10.
u. [2:38] 3:19; 16:31; Lk 3:3.
v. [2:39] Is 57:19; Jl 3:5; Eph 2:17.
w. [2:40] Dt 32:5; Ps 78:8; Lk 9:41; Phil 2:15.
x. [2:41] 2:47; 4:4; 5:14; 6:7; 11:21, 24; 21:20.
y. [2:42–47] 4:32–35.
z. [2:42] 1:14; 6:4.

a. [2:43] 5:12–16.
b. [2:44] 4:32, 34–35.

and to breaking bread in their homes. They ate their meals with exultation and sincerity of heart, **47** praising God and enjoying favor with all the people. And every day the Lord added to their number those who were being saved.

Read Acts 3:1–10

Peter performs a dramatic cure of a lame beggar who has asked for alms.

Reflect: How do I give the gift of faith to others?

Pray: While you may not have the financial resources to help every beggar you meet, you should remember to pray for all who ask for your assistance.

Act: Consider supporting, donating time to, or assisting some type of religious organization that tries to alleviate the plight of the homeless and those who are less fortunate in our society.

Cure of a Crippled Beggar.

3 **1*** Now Peter and John were going up to the temple area for the three o'clock hour of prayer.* **2a** And a man crippled from birth was carried and placed at the gate of the temple called "the Beautiful Gate" every day to beg for alms from the people who entered the temple. **3** When he saw Peter and John about to go into the temple, he asked for alms. **4** But Peter looked intently at him, as did John, and said, "Look at us." **5** He paid attention to them, expecting to receive something from them. **6*b** Peter said, "I have neither silver nor gold, but what I do have I give you: in the name of Jesus Christ the Nazorean, [rise and] walk." **7** Then Peter took him by the right hand and raised him up, and immediately his feet and ankles grew strong. **8c** He leaped up, stood, and walked around, and went into the temple with them, walking and jumping and praising God. **9** When all the people saw him walking and praising God, **10** they recognized him as the one who used to sit begging at the Beautiful Gate of the temple, and they were filled with amazement and astonishment at what had happened to him.

Peter's Speech.

11d As he clung to Peter and John, all the people hurried in amazement toward them in the portico called "Solomon's Portico." **12e** When Peter saw this, he addressed the people, "You Israelites, why are you amazed at this, and why do you look so intently at us as if we had made him walk by our own power or piety? **13f** The God of Abraham, [the God] of Isaac, and [the God] of Jacob, the God of our ancestors, has glorified* his servant Jesus whom you handed over and denied in Pilate's presence, when he had decided to release him. **14g** You denied the Holy and Righteous One* and asked that a murderer be released to you. **15*h** The author of life you put to death, but God raised him from the dead; of this we are witnesses. **16** And by faith in his name, this man, whom you see and know, his name has made strong, and the faith that comes through it has given him this perfect health, in the presence of all of you. **17i** Now I know, brothers, that you acted out of ignorance,* just as your leaders did; **18j** but God has thus brought to fulfillment what he had announced beforehand through the mouth of all the prophets,* that his Messiah would suffer. **19k** Repent, therefore, and be

a. [3:2–8] 14:8–10.
b. [3:6] 4:10.
c. [3:8] Is 35:6; Lk 7:22.
d. [3:11] 5:12; Jn 10:23.
e. [3:12] 14:15.
f. [3:13] Ex 3:6, 15; Is 52:13; Lk 23:14–25.
g. [3:14] Mt 27:20–21; Mk 15:11; Lk 23:18; Jn 18:40.
h. [3:15] 4:10; 5:31 / 1:8; 2:32.
i. [3:17] 13:27; Lk 23:34; 1Cor 2:8; 1Tm 1:13.
j. [3:18] Lk 18:31.
k. [3:19] 2:38.

Read Acts 3:11–26

Peter delivers an expository speech and tries to convince others about the need to repent and be converted.

Reflect: "We are witnesses" (v. 15). What is the significance of these words?

Pray: What aspect of your life needs repentance and conversion? Make this a specific personal prayer intention.

Act: Be conscious of performing a particular action that gives clear witness to the Christian faith.

Read Acts 4:1–22

Peter and John give testimony before the Sanhedrin, where they are questioned regarding their teaching and actions.

Reflect: What is meant by "The stone rejected by you, the builders, ...has become the cornerstone"?

Pray: Being rejected by others is never easy. Pray for those who are experiencing rejection today.

Act: Make a conscious effort to reach out to a person whom you previously rejected.

l. [3:22] 7:37; Dt 18:15, 18.
m. [3:23] Lv 23:29; Dt 18:19.
n. [3:25] Gn 12:3; 18:18; 22:18;
    Sir 44:19–21; Gal 3:8–9.
o. [3:26] 13:46; Rom 1:16.

a. [4:2] 23:6–8; 24:21.
b. [4:8] Mt 10:20.
c. [4:11] Ps 118:22; Is 28:16; Mt 21:42;
    Mk 12:10; Lk 20:17; Rom 9:33; 1Pt 2:7.
d. [4:12] Mt 1:21; 1Cor 3:11.

converted, that your sins may be wiped away, 20 and that the Lord may grant you times of refreshment and send you the Messiah already appointed for you, Jesus,* 21 whom heaven must receive until the times of universal restoration* of which God spoke through the mouth of his holy prophets from of old. 22l For Moses said:*

'A prophet like me will the Lord, your God, raise up for you
from among your own kinsmen;
to him you shall listen in all that he may say to you.
23m Everyone who does not listen to that prophet
will be cut off from the people.'

24 Moreover, all the prophets who spoke, from Samuel and those afterwards, also announced these days. 25n You are the children of the prophets and of the covenant that God made with your ancestors when he said to Abraham, 'In your offspring all the families of the earth shall be blessed.' 26o For you first, God raised up his servant and sent him to bless you by turning each of you from your evil ways."

4 1 While they were still speaking to the people, the priests, the captain of the temple guard, and the Sadducees* confronted them, 2a disturbed that they were teaching the people and proclaiming in Jesus the resurrection of the dead. 3 They laid hands on them and put them in custody until the next day, since it was already evening. 4 But many of those who heard the word came to believe and [the] number of men grew to [about] five thousand.

Before the Sanhedrin.

5 On the next day, their leaders, elders, and scribes were assembled in Jerusalem, 6 with Annas the high priest, Caiaphas, John, Alexander, and all who were of the high-priestly class. 7 They brought them into their presence and questioned them, "By what power or by what name have you done this?" 8b Then Peter, filled with the holy Spirit, answered them, "Leaders of the people and elders: 9 If we are being examined today about a good deed done to a cripple, namely, by what means he was saved, 10 then all of you and all the people of Israel should know that it was in the name of Jesus Christ the Nazorean whom you crucified, whom God raised from the dead; in his name this man stands before you healed. 11c He is 'the stone rejected by you,* the builders, which has become the cornerstone.' 12*d There is no salvation through anyone else, nor is there any other name under heaven

given to the human race by which we are to be saved."

13 Observing the boldness of Peter and John and perceiving them to be uneducated, ordinary men, they were amazed, and they recognized them as the companions of Jesus. 14 Then when they saw the man who had been cured standing there with them, they could say nothing in reply. 15 So they ordered them to leave the Sanhedrin, and conferred with one another, saying, 16 "What are we to do with these men? Everyone living in Jerusalem knows that a remarkable sign was done through them, and we cannot deny it. 17e But so that it may not be spread any further among the people, let us give them a stern warning never again to speak to anyone in this name."

18 So they called them back and ordered them not to speak or teach at all in the name of Jesus. 19f Peter and John, however, said to them in reply, "Whether it is right in the sight of God for us to obey you rather than God, you be the judges. 20 It is impossible for us not to speak about what we have seen and heard." 21 After threatening them further, they released them, finding no way to punish them, on account of the people who were all praising God for what had happened. 22 For the man on whom this sign of healing had been done was over forty years old.

Read Acts 4:23–35

The community thanks God for Peter and John having overcome the threats of the Sanhedrin. A second "Pentecost experience" occurs. The community of believers is described as being "of one heart and mind."

Reflect: How have you experienced a community of believers that is "of one heart and mind"?

Pray: The depiction of unity in the early Christian community does not reflect the situation of Christianity today. Pray for those involved with ecumenism and the work of Christian unity.

Act: Thank God for the support you received from others during a difficult time in your life.

Prayer of the Community.

23 After their release they went back to their own people and reported what the chief priests and elders had told them. 24 And when they heard it, they raised their voices to God with one accord and said, "Sovereign Lord, maker of heaven and earth and the sea and all that is in them, 25g you said by the holy Spirit through the mouth of our father David, your servant:

'Why did the Gentiles rage
    and the peoples entertain folly?
26 The kings of the earth took their stand
    and the princes gathered together
    against the Lord and against his
anointed.'

27h Indeed they gathered in this city against your holy servant Jesus whom you anointed, Herod* and Pontius Pilate, together with the Gentiles and the peoples of Israel, 28 to do what your hand and [your] will had long ago planned to take place. 29 And now, Lord, take note of their threats, and enable your servants to speak your word with all boldness, 30 as you stretch forth [your] hand to heal, and signs and wonders are done through the name of your holy servant Jesus." 31*i As they prayed, the place where they were gathered shook, and they were all filled with the holy Spirit and continued to speak the word of God with boldness.

---

e. [4:17] 5:28.
f. [4:19] 5:29–32.
g. [4:25–26] Ps 2:1–2.
h. [4:27] Lk 23:12–13.
i. [4:31] 2:4.

Life in the Christian Community.

32* The community of believers was of one heart and mind, and no one claimed that any of his possessions was his own, but they had everything in common. **33** With great power the apostles bore witness to the resurrection of the Lord Jesus, and great favor was accorded them all. **34j** There was no needy person among them, for those who owned property or houses would sell them, bring the proceeds of the sale, **35** and put them at the feet of the apostles, and they were distributed to each according to need.

36k Thus Joseph, also named by the apostles Barnabas (which is translated "son of encouragement"), a Levite, a Cypriot by birth, **37** sold a piece of property that he owned, then brought the money and put it at the feet of the apostles.

Ananias and Sapphira.

5 **1*** A man named Ananias, however, with his wife Sapphira, sold a piece of property. **2** He retained for himself, with his wife's knowledge, some of the purchase price, took the remainder, and put it at the feet of the apostles. **3a** But Peter said, "Ananias, why has Satan filled your heart so that you lied to the holy Spirit and retained part of the price of the land? **4** While it remained unsold, did it not remain yours? And when it was sold, was it not still under your control? Why did you contrive this deed? You have lied not to human beings, but to God." **5** When Ananias heard these words, he fell down and breathed his last, and great fear came upon all who heard of it. **6** The young men came and wrapped him up, then carried him out and buried him.

7 After an interval of about three hours, his wife came in, unaware of what had happened. **8** Peter said to her, "Tell me, did you sell the land for this amount?" She answered, "Yes, for that amount." **9** Then Peter said to her, "Why did you agree to test the Spirit of the Lord? Listen, the footsteps of those who have buried your husband are at the door, and they will carry you out." **10** At once, she fell down at his feet and breathed her last. When the young men entered they found her dead, so they carried her out and buried her beside her husband. **11b** And great fear came upon the whole church and upon all who heard of these things.

Signs and Wonders of the Apostles.

12*c Many signs and wonders were done among the people at the hands of the apostles. They were all together in Solomon's portico. **13** None of the others dared to join them, but the people esteemed them. **14** Yet more

j. [4:34–35] 2:44–45.
k. [4:36–37] 9:27; 11:22, 30; 12:25; 13:15; 1Cor 9:6; Gal 2:1, 9, 13; Col 4:10.

a. [5:3] Lk 22:3; Jn 13:2.
b. [5:11] 2:43; 5:5; 19:17.
c. [5:12] 2:43; 6:8; 14:3; 15:12.

than ever, believers in the Lord, great numbers of men and women, were added to them. **15d** Thus they even carried the sick out into the streets and laid them on cots and mats so that when Peter came by, at least his shadow might fall on one or another of them. **16** A large number of people from the towns in the vicinity of Jerusalem also gathered, bringing the sick and those disturbed by unclean spirits, and they were all cured.

Trial before the Sanhedrin.

17*e Then the high priest rose up and all his companions, that is, the party of the Sadducees, and, filled with jealousy, **18** laid hands upon the apostles and put them in the public jail. **19f** But during the night, the angel of the Lord opened the doors of the prison, led them out, and said, **20** "Go and take your place in the temple area, and tell the people everything about this life." **21** When they heard this, they went to the temple early in the morning and taught. When the high priest and his companions arrived, they convened the Sanhedrin, the full senate of the Israelites, and sent to the jail to have them brought in. **22** But the court officers who went did not find them in the prison, so they came back and reported, **23** "We found the jail securely locked and the guards stationed outside the doors, but when we opened them, we found no one inside." **24** When they heard this report, the captain of the temple guard and the chief priests were at a loss about them, as to what this would come to. **25** Then someone came in and reported to them, "The men whom you put in prison are in the temple area and are teaching the people." **26g** Then the captain and the court officers went and brought them in, but without force, because they were afraid of being stoned by the people.

27 When they had brought them in and made them stand before the Sanhedrin, the high priest questioned them, **28h** "We gave you strict orders [did we not?] to stop teaching in that name. Yet you have filled Jerusalem with your teaching and want to bring this man's blood upon us." **29i** But Peter and the apostles said in reply, "We must obey God rather than men. **30*j** The God of our ancestors raised Jesus, though you had him killed by hanging him on a tree. **31k** God exalted him at his right hand* as leader and savior to grant Israel repentance and forgiveness of sins. **32l** We are witnesses of these things, as is the holy Spirit that God has given to those who obey him."

33 When they heard this, they became infuriated and wanted to put them to death. **34*m** But a Pharisee in the Sanhedrin named Gamaliel, a teacher of the law, respected by all the people, stood up, ordered the men to

d. [5:15] 19:11–12; Mk 6:56.
e. [5:17] 4:1–3, 6.
f. [5:19] 12:7–10; 16:25–26.
g. [5:26] Lk 20:19.
h. [5:28] Mt 27:25.
i. [5:29] 4:19.
j. [5:30] 2:23–24.
k. [5:31] 2:38.
l. [5:32] Lk 24:48; Jn 15:26.
m. [5:34] 22:3.

be put outside for a short time, 35 and said to them, "Fellow Israelites, be careful what you are about to do to these men. 36* Some time ago, Theudas appeared, claiming to be someone important, and about four hundred men joined him, but he was killed, and all those who were loyal to him were disbanded and came to nothing. 37 After him came Judas the Galilean at the time of the census. He also drew people after him, but he too perished and all who were loyal to him were scattered. 38 So now I tell you, have nothing to do with these men, and let them go. For if this endeavor or this activi-ty is of human origin, it will destroy itself. 39 But if it comes from God, you will not be able to destroy them; you may even find yourselves fighting against God." They were persuaded by him. 40n After recalling the apostles, they had them flogged, or-dered them to stop speaking in the name of Jesus, and dismissed them. 41o So they left the presence of the Sanhedrin, rejoicing that they had been found worthy to suffer dishonor for the sake of the name. 42p And all day long, both at the temple and in their homes, they did not stop teaching and pro-claiming the Messiah, Jesus.

Read Acts 6:1–7

The community is faced with a practical problem and finds a solu-tion.

Reflect: What created this situa-tion? How was the problem re-solved?

Pray: Those chosen were "filled with the Spirit and wisdom." Pray that in our own day our communi-ties may be able to call on people "filled with the Spirit and wisdom."

Act: Volunteer for some type of service activity as a way to give wit-ness to the Christian faith.

The Need for Assistants.

6 1*a At that time, as the number of disciples contin-ued to grow, the Hellenists complained against the Hebrews because their widows were being neglected in the daily distribution. 2 *So the Twelve called together the community of the disciples and said, "It is not right for us to neglect the word of God to serve at table.* 3 Brothers, select from among you seven reputable men, filled with the Spirit and wisdom, whom we shall appoint to this task, 4 whereas we shall devote ourselves to prayer and to the ministry of the word." 5 The pro-posal was acceptable to the whole community, so they chose Stephen, a man filled with faith and the holy Spir-it, also Philip, Prochorus, Nicanor, Timon, Parmenas, and Nicholas of Antioch, a convert to Judaism. 6b They presented these men to the apostles who prayed and laid hands on them.* 7c The word of God continued to spread, and the number of the disciples in Jerusalem increased greatly; even a large group of priests were be-coming obedient to the faith.

Accusation against Stephen.

8 *Now Stephen, filled with grace and power, was working great wonders and signs among the people. 9 Certain members of the so-called Synagogue of Freedmen, Cyrenians, and Alexandrians, and people from Cilicia and Asia, came forward and debated with Stephen, 10d but they could not withstand the wisdom and the spirit with which he spoke. 11e Then they insti-gated some men to say, "We have heard him speaking blasphemous words against Moses and God." 12 They stirred up the people, the elders, and the scribes, ac-costed him, seized him, and brought him before the Sanhedrin. 13 They presented false witnesses* who tes-tified, "This man never stops saying things against [this]

n. [5:40] Mt 10:17; Acts 4:17–18.
o. [5:41] Mt 5:10–11; 1Pt 4:13.
p. [5:42] 2:46; 5:20–21, 25; 8:35; 17:3; 18:5, 28; 19:4–5.

a. [6:1] 2:45; 4:34–35.
b. [6:6] 1:24; 13:3; 14:23.
c. [6:7] 9:31; 12:24; 16:5; 19:20; 28:30–31.
d. [6:10] Lk 21:15.
e. [6:11] Mt 26:59–61; Mk 14:55–58; Acts 21:21.

Read Acts 6:8—7:53

Stephen's teaching results in his being brought to trial before the Sanhedrin. His testimony there recalls how the promise made to Abraham and his descendants was fulfilled in the events of the exodus.

Reflect: Stephen's speech offers many images from stories in the Old Testament. Choose one of these and reflect on its meaning and significance.

Pray: As a response to the story selected for reflection, pray for a better understanding of lessons learned from the past and how they can be applied to your life today.

Act: Consider how you would explain God's plan of salvation to others.

holy place and the law. [14f] For we have heard him claim that this Jesus the Nazorean will destroy this place and change the customs that Moses handed down to us." [15] All those who sat in the Sanhedrin looked intently at him and saw that his face was like the face of an angel.

Stephen's Discourses.

7 [1] Then the high priest asked, "Is this so?" [2a] And he replied,* "My brothers and fathers, listen. The God of glory appeared to our father Abraham while he was in Mesopotamia,* before he had settled in Haran, [3b] and said to him, 'Go forth from your land and [from] your kinsfolk to the land that I will show you.' [4c] So he went forth from the land of the Chaldeans and settled in Haran. And from there, after his father died, he made him migrate to this land where you now dwell. [5d] Yet he gave him no inheritance in it, not even a foot's length, but he did promise to give it to him and his descendants as a possession, even though he was childless. [6e] And God spoke thus, 'His descendants shall be aliens in a land not their own, where they shall be enslaved and oppressed for four hundred years; [7f] but I will bring judgment on the nation they serve,' God said, 'and after that they will come out and worship me in this place.' [8g] Then he gave him the covenant of circumcision, and so he became the father of Isaac, and circumcised him on the eighth day, as Isaac did Jacob, and Jacob the twelve patriarchs.

[9h] "And the patriarchs, jealous of Joseph, sold him into slavery in Egypt; but God was with him [10i] and rescued him from all his afflictions. He granted him favor and wisdom before Pharaoh, the king of Egypt, who put him in charge of Egypt and [of] his entire household. [11j] Then a famine and great affliction struck all Egypt and Canaan, and our ancestors could find no food; [12k] but when Jacob heard that there was grain in Egypt, he sent our ancestors there a first time. [13l] The second time, Joseph made himself known to his brothers, and Joseph's family became known to Pharaoh. [14m] Then Joseph sent for his father Jacob, inviting him and his whole clan, seventy-five persons; [15n] and Jacob went down to Egypt. And he and our ancestors died [16o] and were brought back to Shechem and placed in the tomb that Abraham had purchased for a sum of money from the sons of Hamor at Shechem.

[17p] "When the time drew near for the fulfillment of the promise that God pledged to Abraham, the people had increased and become very numerous in Egypt, [18q] until another king who knew nothing of Joseph came to power [in Egypt]. [19] He dealt shrewdly with our people and oppressed [our] ancestors by forcing them to ex-

f. [6:14] Mt 26:59–61; 27:40; Jn 2:19.

a. [7:2] Gn 11:31; 12:1; Ps 29:3.
b. [7:3] Gn 12:1.
c. [7:4] Gn 12:5; 15:7.
d. [7:5] Gn 12:7; 13:15; 15:2; 16:1; Dt 2:5.
e. [7:6–7] Gn 15:13–14.
f. [7:7] Ex 3:12.
g. [7:8] Gn 17:10–14; 21:2–4.
h. [7:9] Gn 37:11, 28; 39:2, 3, 21, 23.
i. [7:10] Gn 41:37–43; Ps 105:21; Wis 10:13–14.
j. [7:11] Gn 41:54–57; 42:5.
k. [7:12] Gn 42:1–2.
l. [7:13] Gn 45:3–4, 16.
m. [7:14] Gn 45:9–11, 18–19; 46:27; Ex 1:5 LXX; Dt 10:22.
n. [7:15] Gn 46:5–6; 49:33.
o. [7:16] Gn 23:3–20; 33:19; 49:29–30; 50:13; Jos 24:32.
p. [7:17] Ex 1:7.
q. [7:18] Ex 1:8.

pose their infants, that they might not survive. 20r At this time Moses was born, and he was extremely beautiful. For three months he was nursed in his father's house; 21s but when he was exposed, Pharaoh's daughter adopted him and brought him up as her own son. 22 Moses was educated [in] all the wisdom of the Egyptians and was powerful in his words and deeds.

23t "When he was forty years old, he decided to visit his kinsfolk, the Israelites. 24 When he saw one of them treated unjustly, he defended and avenged the oppressed man by striking down the Egyptian. 25 He assumed [his] kinsfolk would understand that God was offering them deliverance through him, but they did not understand. 26u The next day he appeared to them as they were fighting and tried to reconcile them peacefully, saying, 'Men, you are brothers. Why are you harming one another?' 27 Then the one who was harming his neighbor pushed him aside, saying, 'Who appointed you ruler and judge over us? 28 Are you thinking of killing me as you killed the Egyptian yesterday?' 29v Moses fled when he heard this and settled as an alien in the land of Midian, where he became the father of two sons.

30w "Forty years later, an angel appeared to him in the desert near Mount Sinai in the flame of a burning bush. 31 When Moses saw it, he was amazed at the sight, and as he drew near to look at it, the voice of the Lord came, 32 'I am the God of your fathers, the God of Abraham, of Isaac, and of Jacob.' Then Moses, trembling, did not dare to look at it. 33 But the Lord said to him, 'Remove the sandals from your feet, for the place where you stand is holy ground. 34 I have witnessed the affliction of my people in Egypt and have heard

their groaning, and I have come down to rescue them. Come now, I will send you to Egypt.' 35x This Moses, whom they had rejected with the words, 'Who appointed you ruler and judge?' God sent as [both] ruler and deliverer, through the angel who appeared to him in the bush. 36y This man led them out, performing wonders and signs in the land of Egypt, at the Red Sea, and in the desert for forty years. 37z It was this Moses who said to the Israelites, 'God will raise up for you, from among your own kinsfolk, a prophet like me.' 38a It was he who, in the assembly in the desert, was with the angel who spoke to him on Mount Sinai and with our ancestors, and he received living utterances to hand on to us.

39b "Our ancestors were unwilling to obey him; instead, they pushed him aside and in their hearts turned back to Egypt, 40c saying to Aaron, 'Make us gods who will be our leaders. As for that Moses who led us out of the land of Egypt, we do not know what has happened to him.' 41d So they made a calf in those days, offered sacrifice to the idol, and reveled in the works of their hands. 42e Then God turned and handed them over to worship the host of heaven, as it is written in the book of the prophets:f

'Did you bring me sacrifices and
    offerings
    for forty years in the desert, O
        house of Israel?
43 No, you took up the tent of Moloch
    and the star of [your] god Rephan,
    the images that you made to
        worship.
So I shall take you into exile beyond
    Babylon.'

44g "Our ancestors had the tent of testimony in the desert just as the One who

r. [7:20] Ex 2:2; Heb 11:23.
s. [7:21] Ex 2:3–10.
t. [7:23–24] Ex 2:11–12.
u. [7:26–28] Ex 2:13–14.
v. [7:29] Ex 2:15, 21–22; 18:3–4.
w. [7:30–34] Ex 3:2–3.
x. [7:35] Ex 2:14.
y. [7:36] Ex 7:3, 10; 14:21; Nm 14:33.
z. [7:37] Dt 18:15; Acts 3:22.

a. [7:38] Ex 19:3; 20:1–17; Dt 5:4–22; 6:4–25.
b. [7:39] Nm 14:3.
c. [7:40] Ex 32:1, 23.
d. [7:41] Ex 32:4–6.
e. [7:42–43] Am 5:25–27.
f. [7:42] Jer 7:18; 8:2; 19:13.
g. [7:44] Ex 25:9, 40.

Read Acts 7:54—8:3

In this section we read about the martyrdom of Stephen.

Reflect: Compare this passage with Luke 23:34–46. In what ways do you see Stephen's speech and actions as resembling those of Jesus?

Pray: Pray that, like Stephen, you too will be able to speak and act like Jesus in your own life.

Act: Memorize a phrase from the Bible. Think of an occasion when it might be fitting to speak these words aloud for others to hear.

spoke to Moses directed him to make it according to the pattern he had seen. **45h** Our ancestors who inherited it brought it with Joshua when they dispossessed the nations that God drove out from before our ancestors, up to the time of David, **46i** who found favor in the sight of God and asked that he might find a dwelling place for the house of Jacob. **47j** But Solomon built a house for him. **48k** Yet the Most High does not dwell in houses made by human hands. As the prophet says:

49l 'The heavens are my throne,
      the earth is my footstool.
What kind of house can you build for me?
      says the Lord,
      or what is to be my resting place?
50 Did not my hand make all these things?'

Conclusion.

51 "You stiff-necked people, uncircumcised in heart and ears, you always oppose the holy Spirit; you are just like your ancestors. **52m** Which of the prophets did your ancestors not persecute? They put to death those who foretold the coming of the righteous one, whose betrayers and murderers you have now become. **53n** You received the law as transmitted by angels, but you did not observe it."

Stephen's Martyrdom.

54 When they heard this, they were infuriated, and they ground their teeth at him. **55o** But he, filled with the holy Spirit, looked up intently to heaven and saw the glory of God and Jesus standing at the right hand of God,* **56** and he said, "Behold, I see the heavens opened and the Son of Man standing at the right hand of God." **57** But they cried out in a loud voice, covered their ears,* and rushed upon him together. **58p** They threw him out of the city, and began to stone him. The witnesses laid down their cloaks at the feet of a young man named Saul. **59q** As they were stoning Stephen, he called out, "Lord Jesus, receive my spirit."* **60r** Then he fell to his knees and cried out in a loud voice, "Lord, do not hold this sin against them"; and when he said this, he fell asleep.

h. [7:45] Jos 3:14–17; 18:1; 2Sm 7:5–7.
i. [7:46] 2Sm 7:1–2; 1Kgs 8:17; Ps 132:1–5.
j. [7:47] 1Kgs 6:1; 1Chr 17:12.
k. [7:48] 17:24.
l. [7:49] Is 66:1–2.
m. [7:52] 2Chr 36:16; Mt 23:31, 34.
n. [7:53] Gal 3:19; Heb 2:2.
o. [7:55–56] Mt 26:64; Mk 14:62; Lk 22:69; Acts 2:34.
p. [7:58] 22:20.
q. [7:59] Ps 31:6; Lk 23:46.
r. [7:60] Mt 27:46, 50; Mk 15:34; Lk 23:46.

8 ^{1a} Now Saul was consenting to his exe-cution.

Persecution of the Church.

On that day, there broke out a severe persecution* of the church in Jerusalem, and all were scattered throughout the countryside of Judea and Samaria, except the apostles.* ² Devout men buried Stephen and made a loud lament over him. ^{3b} Saul, meanwhile, was trying to destroy the church;* entering house after house and dragging out men and women, he handed them over for imprisonment.

III: THE MISSION IN JUDEA AND SAMARIA

Read Acts 8:4–40

Philip undertakes a mission to Samaria and Judea. His interactions with Simon the magician and the Ethiopian eunuch are described.

Reflect: To whom and where does the gospel message need to be preached outside the community of believers?

Pray: Pray for contemporary searchers and seekers.

Act: Like Philip, take the time to listen and patiently explain the faith to someone who would like to learn about it.

Phillip in Samaria.

^{4c} Now those who had been scattered went about preaching the word. ^{5d} Thus Philip went down to [the] city of Samaria and proclaimed the Messiah to them. ⁶ With one accord, the crowds paid attention to what was said by Philip when they heard it and saw the signs he was doing. ^{7e} For unclean spirits, crying out in a loud voice, came out of many possessed people, and many paralyzed and crippled people were cured. ⁸ There was great joy in that city.

Simon the Magician.

⁹ A man named Simon used to practice magic* in the city and astounded the people of Samaria, claiming to be someone great. ¹⁰ All of them, from the least to the greatest, paid attention to him, saying, "This man is the 'Power of God' that is called 'Great.'" ¹¹ They paid attention to him because he had astounded them by his magic for a long time, ^{12f} but once they began to believe Philip as he preached the good news about the kingdom of God and the name of Jesus Christ, men and women alike were baptized. ¹³ Even Simon himself believed and, after being baptized, became devoted to Philip; and when he saw the signs and mighty deeds that were occurring, he was astounded.

¹⁴ Now when the apostles in Jerusalem heard that Samaria had accepted the word of God, they sent them Peter and John, ¹⁵ who went down and prayed for them, that they might receive the holy Spirit, ¹⁶ for it had not yet fallen upon any of them; they had only been baptized in the name of the Lord Jesus.* ^{17g} Then they laid hands on them and they received the holy Spirit.

¹⁸ *When Simon saw that the Spirit was conferred by the laying on of the apostles' hands, he offered them money ¹⁹ and said, "Give me this power too, so that anyone upon whom I lay my hands may receive the holy Spirit." ²⁰ But Peter said to him, "May your money perish with you, because you thought that you could

a. [8:1] 22:20.
b. [8:3] 9:1, 13; 22:4; 26:9–11; 1Cor 5:9; Gal 1:13.
c. [8:4] 11:19.
d. [8:5] 6:5; 21:8–9.
e. [8:7] Mk 16:17.
f. [8:12] 1:3; 19:8; 28:23, 31.
g. [8:17] 2:4; 4:31; 10:44–47; 15:8–9; 19:2, 6.

buy the gift of God with money. **21** You have no share or lot in this matter, for your heart is not upright before God. **22** Repent of this wickedness of yours and pray to the Lord that, if possible, your intention may be forgiven. **23** For I see that you are filled with bitter gall and are in the bonds of iniquity." **24** Simon said in reply, "Pray for me to the Lord, that nothing of what you have said may come upon me." **25** So when they had testified and proclaimed the word of the Lord, they returned to Jerusalem and preached the good news to many Samaritan villages.

Philip and the Ethiopian.

26 *Then the angel of the Lord spoke to Philip, "Get up and head south on the road that goes down from Jerusalem to Gaza, the desert route." **27h** So he got up and set out. Now there was an Ethiopian eunuch, a court official of the Candace,* that is, the queen of the Ethiopians, in charge of her entire treasury, who had come to Jerusalem to worship, **28** and was returning home. Seated in his chariot, he was reading the prophet Isaiah. **29** The Spirit said to Philip, "Go and join up with that chariot." **30*** Philip ran up and heard him reading Isaiah the prophet and said, "Do you understand what you are reading?" **31i** He replied, "How can I, unless someone instructs me?" So he in-

vited Philip to get in and sit with him. **32j** This was the scripture passage he was reading:

"Like a sheep he was led to the slaughter,
and as a lamb before its shearer is silent,
so he opened not his mouth.
33 In [his] humiliation justice was denied him.
Who will tell of his posterity?
For his life is taken from the earth."

34 Then the eunuch said to Philip in reply, "I beg you, about whom is the prophet saying this? About himself, or about someone else?" **35** Then Philip opened his mouth and, beginning with this scripture passage, he proclaimed Jesus to him. **36k** As they traveled along the road they came to some water, and the eunuch said, "Look, there is water. What is to prevent my being baptized?" **37 * 38** Then he ordered the chariot to stop, and Philip and the eunuch both went down into the water, and he baptized him. **39l** When they came out of the water, the Spirit of the Lord snatched Philip away, and the eunuch saw him no more, but continued on his way rejoicing. **40m** Philip came to Azotus, and went about proclaiming the good news to all the towns until he reached Caesarea.

Saul's Conversion.

9 **1*a** Now Saul, still breathing murderous threats against the disciples of the Lord, went to the high priest **b** **2** and asked him for letters to the synagogues in Damascus, that, if he should find any men or women who belonged to the Way,* he might bring them back to Jerusalem in chains. **3c** On his journey, as he was nearing Damascus, a light from the sky suddenly flashed around him. **4d** He fell to the ground and heard a voice saying to him, "Saul, Saul, why are you persecuting me?" **5e** He said, "Who are you, sir?" The reply came, "I am Jesus, whom you are persecuting. **6f** Now get up and go into the city and you will be told what you must do." **7g** The men who were traveling with him stood speechless, for they heard the voice but could see no one. **8h** Saul got up from the ground, but when he opened his eyes he could see nothing;* so they led him

h. [8:27] Is 56:3–5.
i. [8:31] Jn 16:13.
j. [8:32–33] Is 53:7–8 LXX.
k. [8:36] 10:47.
l. [8:39] 1Kgs 18:12.
m. [8:40] 21:8.

a. [9:1] 8:3; 9:13; 22:4; 1Cor 15:9; Gal 1:13–14.
b. [9:1–2] 9:14; 26:10.
c. [9:3] 1Cor 9:1; 15:8; Gal 1:16.
d. [9:4] 22:6; 26:14.
e. [9:5] 22:8; 26:15; Mt 25:40.
f. [9:6] 22:10; 26:16.
g. [9:7] 22:9; 26:13–14.
h. [9:8] 22:11.

by the hand and brought him to Damascus. 9 For three days he was unable to see, and he neither ate nor drank.

Saul's Baptism.

10i There was a disciple in Damascus named Ananias, and the Lord said to him in a vision, "Ananias." He answered, "Here I am, Lord." 11j The Lord said to him, "Get up and go to the street called Straight and ask at the house of Judas for a man from Tarsus named Saul. He is there praying, 12 and [in a vision] he has seen a man named Ananias come in and lay [his] hands on him, that he may regain his sight." 13k But Ananias replied, "Lord, I have heard from many sources about this man, what evil things he has done to your holy ones* in Jerusalem. 14l And here he has authority from the chief priests to imprison all who call upon your name." 15m But the Lord said to him, "Go, for this man is a chosen instrument of mine to carry my name before Gentiles, kings, and Israelites, 16 and I will show him what he will have to suffer for my name." 17 So Ananias went and entered the house; laying his hands on him, he said, "Saul, my brother, the Lord has sent me, Jesus who appeared to you on the way by which you came, that you may regain your sight and be filled with the holy Spirit." 18 Immediately things like scales fell from his eyes and he regained his sight. He got up and was baptized, 19 and when he had eaten, he recovered his strength.*

Saul Preaches in Damascus.

He stayed some days with the disciples in Damascus, 20 and he began at once to proclaim Jesus in the synagogues, that he is the Son of God.* 21 All who heard him were astounded and said, "Is not this the man who in Jerusalem ravaged those who call upon this name, and came here expressly to take them back in chains to the chief priests?" 22 But Saul grew all the stronger and confounded [the] Jews who lived in Damascus, proving that this is the Messiah.

Saul Visits Jerusalem.

23 After a long time had passed, the Jews conspired to kill him, 24n but their plot became known to Saul. Now they were keeping watch on the gates day and night so as to kill him, 25 but his disciples took him one night and let him down through an opening in the wall, lowering him in a basket.

26o When he arrived in Jerusalem* he tried to join the disciples, but they were all afraid of him, not believing that he was a disciple. 27 Then Barnabas took charge of

i. [9:10–19] 22:12–16.
j. [9:11] 21:39.
k. [9:13] 8:3; 9:1.
l. [9:14] 9:1–2; 26:10; 1Cor 1:2; 2Tm 2:22.
m. [9:15] 22:15; 26:1; 27:24.
n. [9:24–25] 2Cor 11:32–33.
o. [9:26–27] Gal 1:18.

Read Acts 9:19b–30

Saul spends time in Damascus and confounds others by the radical change he has undergone. Barnabas introduces Saul to the apostles in Jerusalem.

Reflect: Why is it difficult to accept someone whose life has changed?

Pray: Acceptance of change in ourselves or in others is not easy. Ask for God's help in changing the aspects of your life that need conversion. Pray that you may have the willingness to welcome and accept someone who is in recovery or has gone through a major life change.

Act: Like Barnabas, take the initiative to introduce a person who is unknown to others. Speak favorably and in a positive way about this individual and help him or her feel welcome.

Read Acts 9:31–43

Peter performs healing miracles in Lydda and Joppa.

Reflect: How are these two healing stories similar to other healing accounts in the Bible?

Pray: Many people suffer from various ailments, afflictions, and forms of sickness. Remember in your prayers those who are ill or in pain.

Act: Do an act of kindness as a way of bringing God's healing touch to a person who is sick or suffering.

him and brought him to the apostles, and he reported to them how on the way he had seen the Lord and that he had spoken to him, and how in Damascus he had spoken out boldly in the name of Jesus. 28 He moved about freely with them in Jerusalem, and spoke out boldly in the name of the Lord. 29 He also spoke and debate with the Hellenists,* but they tried to kill him. 30p And when the brothers learned of this, they took him down to Caesarea and sent him on his way to Tarsus.

The Church at Peace.

31 *The church throughout all Judea, Galilee, and Samaria was at peace. It was being built up and walked in the fear of the Lord, and with the consolation of the holy Spirit it grew in numbers.

Peter Heals Aeneas at Lydda.

32 As Peter was passing through every region, he went down to the holy ones living in Lydda. 33 There he found a man named Aeneas, who had been confined to bed for eight years, for he was paralyzed. 34 Peter said to him, "Aeneas, Jesus Christ heals you. Get up and make your bed." He got up at once. 35 And all the inhabitants of Lydda and Sharon saw him, and they turned to the Lord.

Peter Restores Tabitha to Life.

36 Now in Joppa there was a disciple named Tabitha (which translated means Dorcas).* She was completely occupied with good deeds and almsgiving. 37 Now during those days she fell sick and died, so after washing her, they laid [her] out in a room upstairs. 38 Since Lydda was near Joppa, the disciples, hearing that Peter was there, sent two men to him with the request, "Please come to us without delay." 39 So Peter got up and went with them. When he arrived, they took him to the room upstairs where all the widows came to him weeping and showing him the tunics and cloaks that Dorcas had made while she was with them. 40q Peter sent them all out and knelt down and prayed. Then he turned to her body and said, "Tabitha, rise up." She opened her eyes, saw Peter, and sat up. 41 He gave her his hand and raised her up, and when he had called the holy ones and the widows, he presented her alive. 42 This became known all over Joppa, and many came to believe in the Lord. 43*r And he stayed a long time in Joppa with Simon, a tanner.

p. [9:30] 11:25.
q. [9:40] Mk 5:40–41.
r. [9:43] 10:6.

IV: THE INAUGURATION OF THE GENTILE MISSION

Read Acts 10:1–33

During prayer, both Cornelius and Peter experience profound visions that offer new insights into their lives.

Reflect: Why is it important to grow in our faith by broadening our vision?

Pray: Accepting people with different faith insights is not always easy. Offer a prayer asking for God's help to be open to new and different possibilities.

Act: Let go of something from the past, a previously held understanding that needs to be changed.

The Vision of Cornelius.

10 1*a Now in Caesarea there was a man named Cornelius, a centurion of the Cohort called the Italica,* 2 devout and God-fearing along with his whole household, who used to give alms generously* to the Jewish people and pray to God constantly. 3 One afternoon about three o'clock,* he saw plainly in a vision an angel of God come in to him and say to him, "Cornelius." 4 He looked intently at him and, seized with fear, said, "What is it, sir?" He said to him, "Your prayers and almsgiving have ascended as a memorial offering before God. 5 Now send some men to Joppa and summon one Simon who is called Peter. 6b He is staying with another Simon, a tanner, who has a house by the sea." 7 When the angel who spoke to him had left, he called two of his servants and a devout soldier* from his staff, 8 explained everything to them, and sent them to Joppa.

The Vision of Peter.

9* The next day, while they were on their way and nearing the city, Peter went up to the roof terrace to pray at about noontime.* 10 He was hungry and wished to eat, and while they were making preparations he fell into a trance. 11c He saw heaven opened and something resembling a large sheet coming down, lowered to the ground by its four corners. 12 In it were all the earth's four-legged animals and reptiles and the birds of the sky. 13 A voice said to him, "Get up, Peter. Slaughter and eat." 14d But Peter said, "Certainly not, sir. For never have I eaten anything profane and unclean." 15e The voice spoke to him again, a second time, "What God has made clean, you are not to call profane." 16 This happened three times, and then the object was taken up into the sky.

17* While Peter was in doubt about the meaning of the vision he had seen, the men sent by Cornelius asked for Simon's house and arrived at the entrance. 18 They called out inquiring whether Simon, who is called Peter, was staying there. 19f As Peter was pondering the vision, the Spirit said [to him], "There are three men here looking for you. 20 So get up, go downstairs, and accompany them without hesitation, because I have sent them." 21 Then Peter went down to the men and said, "I am the one you are looking for. What is the reason for your being here?" 22g They answered, "Cornelius, a centurion, an upright and God-fearing man, respected by the whole Jewish nation, was directed by a holy angel to

a. [10:1–8] 10:30–33.
b. [10:6] 9:43.
c. [10:11–20] 11:5–12.
d. [10:14] Lv 11:1–47; Ez 4:14.
e. [10:15] Mk 7:15–19; Gal 2:12.
f. [10:19] 13:2.
g. [10:22] Lk 7:4–5.

Read Acts 10:34–49

Peter's speech to the household of Cornelius reflects a new understanding of the outreach mission of the early Christian community.

Reflect: Why is the phrase "God shows no partiality" the core of Peter's speech?

Pray: Missionaries devote their lives to proclaiming the gospel message. Prayerfully support missionaries in their efforts.

Act: Those who are not Christian often lead Christian lives. Think about some people you know who exemplify this and consider what you can learn from them.

summon you to his house and to hear what you have to say." 23 So he invited them in and showed them hospitality.

The next day he got up and went with them, and some of the brothers from Joppa went with him. 24* On the following day he entered Caesarea. Cornelius was expecting them and had called together his relatives and close friends. 25h When Peter entered, Cornelius met him and, falling at his feet, paid him homage. 26 Peter, however, raised him up, saying, "Get up. I myself am also a human being." 27 While he conversed with him, he went in and found many people gathered together 28i and said to them, "You know that it is unlawful for a Jewish man to associate with, or visit, a Gentile, but God has shown me that I should not call any person profane or unclean.* 29 And that is why I came without objection when sent for. May I ask, then, why you summoned me?"

30 Cornelius replied, "Four days ago* at this hour, three o'clock in the afternoon, I was at prayer in my house when suddenly a man in dazzling robes stood before me and said, 31 'Cornelius, your prayer has been heard and your almsgiving remembered before God. 32 Send therefore to Joppa and summon Simon, who is called Peter. He is a guest in the house of Simon, a tanner, by the sea.' 33 So I sent for you immediately, and you were kind enough to come. Now therefore we are all here in the presence of God to listen to all that you have been commanded by the Lord."

Peter's Speech.

34*j Then Peter proceeded to speak and said,* "In truth, I see that God shows no partiality. 35 Rather, in every nation whoever fears him and acts uprightly is acceptable to him. 36*k You know the word [that] he sent to the Israelites as he proclaimed peace through Jesus Christ, who is Lord of all,* 37l what has happened all over Judea, beginning in Galilee after the baptism that John preached, 38m how God anointed Jesus of Nazareth* with the holy Spirit and power. He went about doing good and healing all those oppressed by the devil, for God was with him. 39 We are witnesses* of all that he did both in the country of the Jews and [in] Jerusalem. They put him to death by hanging him on a tree. 40 This man God raised [on] the third day and granted that he be visible, 41n not to all the people, but to us, the witnesses chosen by God in advance, who ate and drank with him after he rose from the dead. 42o He commissioned us to preach to the people and testify that he is the one appointed by God as judge of the living and the dead.* 43 To him all the prophets bear witness, that

h. [10:25–26] 14:13–15; Rev 19:10.
i. [10:28] Gal 2:11–16.
j. [10:34] Dt 17:2; 2Chr 19:7; Jb 34:19; Wis 6:7; Rom 2:11; Gal 2:6; Eph 6:9; 1Pt 1:17.
k. [10:36] Is 52:7; Na 2:1.
l. [10:37] Mt 4:12; Mk 1:14; Lk 4:14.
m. [10:38] Is 61:1; Lk 4:18.
n. [10:41] Lk 24:41–43.
o. [10:42] 1:8; 3:15; 17:31; Lk 24:48; Rom 14:9; 2Tm 4:1.

Read Acts 11:1–18

Peter uses his recent vision to explain his actions in welcoming Gentiles.

Reflect: How is the outpouring of the Spirit on the Gentiles similar to what occurred during the Pentecost event?

Pray: Pray for an outpouring of the Spirit to enable you to see life in a new way.

Act: Like Peter, be willing to allow a new spiritual insight to change your attitude toward others and the way you treat them.

everyone who believes in him will receive forgiveness of sins through his name."

The Baptism of Cornelius.

44p While Peter was still speaking these things, the holy Spirit fell upon all who were listening to the word.* **45** The circumcised believers who had accompanied Peter were astounded that the gift of the holy Spirit should have been poured out on the Gentiles also, **46** for they could hear them speaking in tongues and glorifying God. Then Peter responded, **47q** "Can anyone withhold the water for baptizing these people, who have received the holy Spirit even as we have?" **48** He ordered them to be baptized in the name of Jesus Christ. **49** Then they invited him to stay for a few days.

The Baptism of the Gentiles Explained.

11 **1** *Now the apostles and the brothers who were in Judea heard that the Gentiles too had accepted the word of God. **2** So when Peter went up to Jerusalem the circumcised believers confronted him, **3** saying, "You entered* the house of uncircumcised people and ate with them." **4** Peter began and explained it to them step by step, saying, **5a** "I was at prayer in the city of Joppa when in a trance I had a vision, something resembling a large sheet coming down, lowered from the sky by its four corners, and it came to me. **6** Looking intently into it, I observed and saw the four-legged animals of the earth, the wild beasts, the reptiles, and the birds of the sky. **7** I also heard a voice say to me, 'Get up, Peter. Slaughter and eat.' **8** But I said, 'Certainly not, sir, because nothing profane or unclean has ever entered my mouth.' **9** But a second time a voice from heaven answered, 'What God has made clean, you are not to call profane.' **10** This happened three times, and then everything was drawn up again into the sky. **11** Just then three men appeared at the house where we were, who had been sent to me from Caesarea. **12** The Spirit told me to accompany them without discriminating. These six brothers* also went with me, and we entered the man's house. **13b** He related to us how he had seen [the] angel standing in his house, saying, 'Send someone to Joppa and summon Simon, who is called Peter, **14** who will speak words to you by which you and all your household will be saved.' **15c** As I began to speak, the holy Spirit fell upon them as it had upon us at the beginning, **16d** and I remembered the word of the Lord, how he had said, 'John baptized with water but you will be baptized with the holy Spirit.' **17e** If then God gave them the same gift he gave to us when we came to believe in the Lord Jesus Christ, who was I to be able to

p. [10:44] 11:15; 15:8.
q. [10:47] 8:36.

a. [11:5–12] 10:11–20.
b. [11:13] 10:3–5, 22, 30–32.
c. [11:15] 10:44.
d. [11:16] 1:5; 19:4; Lk 3:16.
e. [11:17] 15:8–9.

Read Acts 11:19–30

The early church continues to grow, expanding with Gentile converts in Antioch. Barnabas is sent from Jerusalem to investigate. He goes to Tarsus seeking Saul and brings him back to Antioch, where the disciples are called Christians for the first time.

Reflect: What is the significance of being called Christians?

Pray: In our own day too the church continues to grow, expand, and increase in numbers. Pray for those who are considering becoming Christians, especially those who will face difficulties as a result of making this decision.

Act: Following the example of the community in Antioch that assisted the Jerusalem community in time of need, consider supporting some type of foreign mission endeavor.

Read Acts 12:1–23

King Herod has James, the brother of John, put to death and has Peter imprisoned. Peter's unexpected deliverance from prison results in a humorous scene with a maid named Rhoda. We also learn of Herod's gruesome death.

Reflect: What accounts for Rhoda's behavior?

Pray: Humor can sometimes help during difficult and stressful moments. Pray for the ability to laugh and enjoy life as a way of alleviating life's tensions and struggles.

Act: See if you can find some areas of your life in which humor could play a more significant role.

f. [11:19] 8:1–4.
g. [11:28] 21:10.
h. [11:29–30] 12:25.

a. [12:5] Jas 5:16.

hinder God?" [18] When they heard this, they stopped objecting and glorified God, saying, "God has then granted life-giving repentance to the Gentiles too."

The Church at Antioch.

[19]*f Now those who had been scattered by the persecution that arose because of Stephen went as far as Phoenicia, Cyprus, and Antioch, preaching the word to no one but Jews. [20] There were some Cypriots and Cyrenians among them, however, who came to Antioch and began to speak to the Greeks as well, proclaiming the Lord Jesus. [21] The hand of the Lord was with them and a great number who believed turned to the Lord. [22] The news about them reached the ears of the church in Jerusalem, and they sent Barnabas [to go] to Antioch. [23] When he arrived and saw the grace of God, he rejoiced and encouraged them all to remain faithful to the Lord in firmness of heart, [24] for he was a good man, filled with the holy Spirit and faith. And a large number of people was added to the Lord. [25] Then he went to Tarsus to look for Saul, [26] and when he had found him he brought him to Antioch. For a whole year they met with the church and taught a large number of people, and it was in Antioch that the disciples were first called Christians.*

The Prediction of Agabus.

[27]* At that time some prophets came down from Jerusalem to Antioch, [28]g and one of them named Agabus stood up and predicted by the Spirit that there would be a severe famine all over the world, and it happened under Claudius. [29]h So the disciples determined that, according to ability, each should send relief to the brothers who lived in Judea. [30]* This they did, sending it to the presbyters in care of Barnabas and Saul.

Herod's Persecution of the Christians.

12 [1]* About that time King Herod laid hands upon some members of the church to harm them. [2] He had James, the brother of John,* killed by the sword, [3]* and when he saw that this was pleasing to the Jews he proceeded to arrest Peter also. (It was [the] feast of Unleavened Bread.) [4] He had him taken into custody and put in prison under the guard of four squads of four soldiers each. He intended to bring him before the people after Passover. [5]a Peter thus was being kept in prison, but prayer by the church was fervently being made to God on his behalf.

[6] On the very night before Herod was to bring him to trial, Peter, secured by double chains, was sleeping be-

tween two soldiers, while outside the door guards kept watch on the prison. [7] Suddenly the angel of the Lord stood by him and a light shone in the cell. He tapped Peter on the side and awakened him, saying, "Get up quickly." The chains fell from his wrists. [8] The angel said to him, "Put on your belt and your sandals." He did so. Then he said to him, "Put on your cloak and follow me." [9] So he followed him out, not realizing that what was happening through the angel was real; he thought he was seeing a vision. [10] They passed the first guard, then the second, and came to the iron gate leading out to the city, which opened for them by itself. They emerged and made their way down an alley, and suddenly the angel left him. [11] Then Peter recovered his senses and said, "Now I know for certain that [the] Lord sent his angel and rescued me from the hand of Herod and from all that the Jewish people had been expecting." [12b] When he realized this, he went to the house of Mary, the mother of John who is called Mark, where there were many people gathered in prayer. [13] When he knocked on the gateway door, a maid named Rhoda came to answer it. [14] She was so overjoyed when she recognized Peter's voice that, instead of opening the gate, she ran in and announced that Peter was standing at the gate. [15] They told her, "You are out of your mind," but she insisted that it was so. But they kept saying, "It is his angel." [16] But Peter continued to knock, and when they opened it, they saw him and were astounded. [17] He motioned to them with his hand to be quiet and explained [to them] how the Lord had led him out of the prison, and said, "Report this to James* and the brothers." Then he left and went to another place. [18c] At daybreak there was no small commotion among the soldiers over what had become of Peter. [19] Herod, after instituting a search but not finding him, ordered the guards tried and executed. Then he left Judea to spend some time in Caesarea.

Herod's Death.

[20] *He had long been very angry with the people of Tyre and Sidon, who now came to him in a body. After winning over Blastus, the king's chamberlain, they sued for peace because their country was supplied with food from the king's territory. [21] On an appointed day, Herod, attired in royal robes, [and] seated on the rostrum, addressed them publicly. [22] The assembled crowd cried out, "This is the voice of a god, not of a man." [23] At once the angel of the Lord struck him down because he did not ascribe the honor to God, and he was eaten by worms and breathed his last. [24d] But the word of God continued to spread and grow.

b. [12:12] 12:25; 15:37.
c. [12:18] 5:22–24.
d. [12:24] 6:7.

Read Acts 13:13–43

Paul arrives with his companions in Antioch of Pisidia and delivers a major sermon at the synagogue.

Reflect: Compare Paul's address in Acts 13:16–41 with Peter's Pentecost speech in Acts 2:14–40.

Pray: As this address notes, our faith has Jewish roots. Pray especially for better understanding between Jews and Christians.

Act: Learn something new and specific about Judaism as a way to better understand our spiritual kinship.

Mission of Barnabas and Saul.

25e After Barnabas and Saul completed their relief mission, they returned to Jerusalem,* taking with them John, who is called Mark.

13 1* Now there were in the church at Antioch prophets and teachers: Barnabas, Symeon who was called Niger, Lucius of Cyrene, Manaen who was a close friend of Herod the tetrarch, and Saul. 2 While they were worshiping the Lord and fasting, the holy Spirit said, "Set apart for me Barnabas and Saul for the work to which I have called them." 3 Then, completing their fasting and prayer, they laid hands on them and sent them off.

First Mission Begins in Cyprus.

4* So they, sent forth by the holy Spirit, went down to Seleucia and from there sailed to Cyprus. 5 When they arrived in Salamis, they proclaimed the word of God in the Jewish synagogues. They had John* also as their assistant. 6 When they had traveled through the whole island as far as Paphos, they met a magician named Bar-Jesus who was a Jewish false prophet.* 7 He was with the proconsul Sergius Paulus, a man of intelligence, who had summoned Barnabas and Saul and wanted to hear the word of God. 8 But Elymas the magician (for that is what his name means) opposed them in an attempt to turn the proconsul away from the faith. 9 But Saul, also known as Paul,* filled with the holy Spirit, looked intently at him 10 and said, "You son of the devil, you enemy of all that is right, full of every sort of deceit and fraud. Will you not stop twisting the straight paths of [the] Lord? 11 Even now the hand of the Lord is upon you. You will be blind, and unable to see the sun for a time." Immediately a dark mist fell upon him, and he went about seeking people to lead him by the hand. 12 When the proconsul saw what had happened, he came to believe, for he was astonished by the teaching about the Lord.

Paul's Arrival at Antioch in Pisidia.

13a From Paphos, Paul and his companions set sail and arrived at Perga in Pamphylia. But John left them and returned to Jerusalem. 14 They continued on from Perga and reached Antioch in Pisidia. On the sabbath they entered [into] the synagogue and took their seats. 15 After the reading of the law and the prophets, the synagogue officials sent word to them, "My brothers, if one of you has a word of exhortation for the people, please speak."

e. [12:25] 11:29–30.

a. [13:13] 15:38.

Paul's Address in the Synagogue.

16 *So Paul got up, motioned with his hand, and said, "Fellow Israelites and you others who are God-fearing,* listen. 17b The God of this people Israel chose our ancestors and exalted the people during their sojourn in the land of Egypt. With uplifted arm he led them out of it 18c and for about forty years he put up with* them in the desert. 19d When he had destroyed seven nations in the land of Canaan, he gave them their land as an inheritance 20e at the end of about four hundred and fifty years.* After these things he provided judges up to Samuel [the] prophet. 21f Then they asked for a king. God gave them Saul, son of Kish, a man from the tribe of Benjamin, for forty years. 22g Then he removed him and raised up David as their king; of him he testified, 'I have found David, son of Jesse, a man after my own heart; he will carry out my every wish.' 23h From this man's descendants God, according to his promise, has brought to Israel a savior, Jesus. 24i John heralded his coming by proclaiming a baptism of repentance to all the people of Israel; 25j and as John was completing his course, he would say, 'What do you suppose that I am? I am not he. Behold, one is coming after me; I am not worthy to unfasten the sandals of his feet.'

26 "My brothers, children of the family of Abraham, and those others among you who are God-fearing, to us this word of salvation has been sent. 27 The inhabitants of Jerusalem and their leaders failed to recognize him, and by condemning him they fulfilled the oracles of the prophets that are read sabbath after sabbath. 28k For even though they found no grounds for a death sentence, they asked Pilate to have him put to death, 29l and when they had accomplished all that was written about him, they took him down from the tree and placed him in a tomb. 30m But God raised him from the dead, 31n and for many days he appeared to those who had come up with him from Galilee to Jerusalem. These are [now] his witnesses before the people.* 32 We ourselves are proclaiming this good news to you that what God promised our ancestors 33o he has brought to fulfillment for us, [their] children, by raising up Jesus, as it is written in the second psalm, 'You are my son; this day I have begotten you.' 34p And that he raised him from the dead never to return to corruption he declared in this way, 'I shall give you the benefits assured to David.' 35q That is why he also says in another psalm, 'You will not suffer your holy one to see corruption.' 36r Now David, after he had served the will of God in his lifetime, fell asleep, was gathered to his ancestors, and did see corruption. 37 But the one whom God raised up did not see corruption. 38 You must know, my brothers, that through him forgiveness of sins is being proclaimed to you, [and] in regard to everything from which you could not be justified* under the law of Moses, 39s in him every believer is justified. 40 Be careful, then, that what was said in the prophets not come about:

41t 'Look on, you scoffers,
    be amazed and disappear.
For I am doing a work in your days,
    a work that you will never believe
    even if someone tells you.'"

42 As they were leaving, they invited them to speak on these subjects the following sabbath. 43 After the congregation had dis-

b. [13:17] Ex 6:1, 6; 12:51.
c. [13:18] Ex 16:1, 35; Nm 14:34.
d. [13:19] Dt 7:1; Jos 14:1–2.
e. [13:20] Jgs 2:16; 1Sm 3:20.
f. [13:21] 1Sm 8:5, 19; 9:16; 10:1, 20–21, 24; 11:15.
g. [13:22] 1Sm 13:14; 16:12–13; Ps 89:20–21.
h. [13:23] Is 11:1.
i. [13:24] Mt 3:1–2; Mk 1:4–5; Lk 3:2–3.
j. [13:25] Mt 3:11; Mk 1:7; Lk 3:16; Jn 1:20, 27.
k. [13:28] Mt 27:20, 22–23; Mk 15:13–14; Lk 23:4, 14–15, 21–23; Jn 19:4–6, 15.

l. [13:29] Mt 27:59–60; Mk 15:46; Lk 23:53; Jn 19:38, 41–42.
m. [13:30] 2:24, 32; 3:15; 4:10; 17:31.
n. [13:31] 1:3, 8; 10:39, 41; Mt 28:8–10, 16–20; Mk 16:9, 12–20; Lk 24:13–53; Jn 20:11–29; 21:1–23.
o. [13:33] Ps 2:7.
p. [13:34] Is 55:3.
q. [13:35] Ps 16:10.
r. [13:36] 2:29; 1Kgs 2:10.
s. [13:39] Rom 3:20.
t. [13:41] Heb 1:5.

Read Acts 13:44–52
Paul and Barnabas experience rejection and turn their attention to proclaiming the gospel message to the Gentiles.

Reflect: Compare this passage with the verses describing the presentation of the infant Jesus in the temple (Lk 2:25–35). Notice the similarities, such as mention of rejection, suffering, and "the light to the Gentiles."

Pray: Pray that you may be "an instrument of salvation to the ends of the earth."

Act: Be willing to speak about your faith in a setting that is not easy.

Read Acts 14:1–20
Paul and Barnabas continue their mission in Iconium, Lystra, and Derbe. While performing a miraculous cure in Lystra, they are misidentified as Greek gods.

Reflect: Think about the humor associated with this misidentification of Paul and Barnabas. What was the scene like?

Pray: The missionaries Paul and Barnabas spoke boldly in proclaiming the Christian faith. Pray that you may have the same sense of boldness.

Act: Exhibit Paul's spirit by "getting up" and moving on to the next challenge when facing personal adversity.

---

persed, many Jews and worshipers who were converts to Judaism followed Paul and Barnabas, who spoke to them and urged them to remain faithful to the grace of God.

Address to the Gentiles.

44 On the following sabbath almost the whole city gathered to hear the word of the Lord. **45** When the Jews saw the crowds, they were filled with jealousy and with violent abuse contradicted what Paul said. **46u** Both Paul and Barnabas spoke out boldly and said, "It was necessary that the word of God be spoken to you first, but since you reject it and condemn yourselves as unworthy of eternal life, we now turn to the Gentiles.* **47v** For so the Lord has commanded us, 'I have made you a light to the Gentiles, that you may be an instrument of salvation to the ends of the earth.'"

48 The Gentiles were delighted when they heard this and glorified the word of the Lord. All who were destined for eternal life came to believe, **49** and the word of the Lord continued to spread through the whole region. **50** The Jews, however, incited the women of prominence who were worshipers and the leading men of the city, stirred up a persecution against Paul and Barnabas, and expelled them from their territory. **51w** So they shook the dust from their feet in protest against them and went to Iconium.* **52** The disciples were filled with joy and the holy Spirit.

Paul and Barnabas at Iconium.

14 **1** In Iconium they entered the Jewish synagogue together and spoke in such a way that a great number of both Jews and Greeks came to believe, **2** although the disbelieving Jews stirred up and poisoned the minds of the Gentiles against the brothers. **3a** So they stayed for a considerable period, speaking out boldly for the Lord, who confirmed the word about his grace by granting signs and wonders to occur through their hands. **4** The people of the city were divided: some were with the Jews; others, with the apostles. **5b** When there was an attempt by both the Gentiles and the Jews, together with their leaders, to attack and stone them, **6** they realized it and fled to the Lycaonian cities of Lystra and Derbe and to the surrounding countryside, **7** where they continued to proclaim the good news.

Paul and Barnabas at Lystra.

8 *At Lystra there was a crippled man, lame from birth, who had never walked. **9** He listened to Paul speaking, who looked intently at him, saw that he had the faith to be healed, **10** and called out in a loud voice,

---

u. [13:46] 3:26; Rom 1:16.
v. [13:47] Is 49:6.
w. [13:51] Mt 10:14; Mk 6:11; Lk 9:5; 10:11.

a. [14:3] Mk 16:17–20.
b. [14:5] 2Tm 3:11.

"Stand up straight on your feet." He jumped up and began to walk about. **11c** When the crowds saw what Paul had done, they cried out in Lycaonian, "The gods have come down to us in human form." **12** They called Barnabas "Zeus"* and Paul "Hermes," because he was the chief speaker. **13** And the priest of Zeus, whose temple was at the entrance to the city, brought oxen and garlands to the gates, for he together with the people intended to offer sacrifice.

14 The apostles Barnabas and Paul tore their garments* when they heard this and rushed out into the crowd, shouting, **15*d** "Men, why are you doing this? We are of the same nature as you, human beings. We proclaim to you good news that you should turn from these idols to the living God, 'who made heaven and earth and sea and all that is in them.' **16e** In past generations he allowed all Gentiles to go their own ways; **17f** yet, in bestowing his goodness, he did not leave himself without witness, for he gave you rains from heaven and fruitful seasons, and filled you with nourishment and gladness for your hearts." **18** Even with these words, they scarcely restrained the crowds from offering sacrifice to them.

19g However, some Jews from Antioch and Iconium arrived and won over the crowds. They stoned Paul and dragged him out of the city, supposing that he was dead. **20** But when the disciples gathered around him, he got up and entered the city. On the following day he left with Barnabas for Derbe.

End of the First Mission.

21 After they had proclaimed the good news to that city and made a considerable number of disciples, they returned to Lystra and to Iconium and to Antioch. **22h** They strengthened the spirits of the disciples and exhorted them to persevere in the faith, saying, "It is necessary for us to undergo many hardships to enter the kingdom of God." **23** They appointed presbyters* for them in each church and, with prayer and fasting, commended them to the Lord in whom they had put their faith. **24** Then they traveled through Pisidia and reached Pamphylia. **25** After proclaiming the word at Perga they went down to Attalia. **26i** From there they sailed to Antioch, where they had been commended to the grace of God for the work they had now accomplished. **27** And when they arrived, they called the church together and reported what God had done with them and how he had opened the door of faith to the Gentiles. **28** Then they spent no little time with the disciples.

c. [14:11] 28:6.
d. [14:15] 3:12; 10:26; Ex 20:11; Ps 146:6.
e. [14:16] 17:30.
f. [14:17] Wis 13:1.
g. [14:19–20] 2Cor 11:25; 2Tm 3:11.
h. [14:22] 1Thes 3:3.
i. [14:26] 13:1–3.

Read Acts 15:1–21

The issue of how to accept Gentile converts is addressed in Jerusalem, with Paul and Barnabas sent as representatives from Antioch. James speaks about dietary laws.

Reflect: Notice how this controversy among the early Christians is resolved.

Pray: People are often judged on the basis of external appearance and actions. Pray that you will not be tempted to be judgmental of others.

Act: Take a positive step or specific action to make a new beginning in some area of your life that needs to change.

Council of Jerusalem.

15 ¹*ᵃ Some who had come down from Judea were instructing the brothers, "Unless you are circumcised according to the Mosaic practice, you cannot be saved."*ᵇ ² Because there arose no little dissension and debate by Paul and Barnabas with them, it was decided that Paul, Barnabas, and some of the others should go up to Jerusalem to the apostles and presbyters about this question. ³ They were sent on their journey by the church, and passed through Phoenicia and Samaria telling of the conversion of the Gentiles, and brought great joy to all the brothers. ⁴ When they arrived in Jerusalem, they were welcomed by the church, as well as by the apostles and the presbyters, and they reported what God had done with them. ⁵ But some from the party of the Pharisees who had become believers stood up and said, "It is necessary to circumcise them and direct them to observe the Mosaic law."

⁶* The apostles and the presbyters met together to see about this matter. ⁷*ᶜ After much debate had taken place, Peter got up and said to them, "My brothers, you are well aware that from early days God made his choice among you that through my mouth the Gentiles would hear the word of the gospel and believe. ⁸ᵈ And God, who knows the heart, bore witness by granting them the holy Spirit just as he did us. ⁹ᵉ He made no distinction between us and them, for by faith he purified their hearts. ¹⁰ᶠ Why, then, are you now putting God to the test by placing on the shoulders of the disciples a yoke that neither our ancestors nor we have been able to bear? ¹¹ᵍ On the contrary, we believe that we are saved through the grace of the Lord Jesus, in the same way as they."* ¹² The whole assembly fell silent, and they listened while Paul and Barnabas described the signs and wonders God had worked among the Gentiles through them.

James on Dietary Law.

¹³* After they had fallen silent, James responded, "My brothers, listen to me. ¹⁴ Symeon* has described how God first concerned himself with acquiring from among the Gentiles a people for his name. ¹⁵ The words of the prophets agree with this, as is written:

¹⁶ʰ 'After this I shall return
   and rebuild the fallen hut of David;
from its ruins I shall rebuild it
   and raise it up again,
¹⁷ so that the rest of humanity may seek out the Lord,
   even all the Gentiles on whom my name is invoked.
Thus says the Lord who accomplishes these things,
   ¹⁸ known from of old.'

a. [15:1–4] Gal 2:1–9.
b. [15:1] Lv 12:3; Gal 5:2.
c. [15:7] 10:27–43.
d. [15:8] 10:44–48.
e. [15:9] 10:34–35.
f. [15:10] Mt 23:4; Gal 5:1.
g. [15:11] Gal 2:16; 3:11; Eph 2:5–8.
h. [15:16–17] Am 9:11–12.

Read Acts 15:22–35

An agreement is reached in resolving an important early church issue. A letter is written and Judas (Barsabbas) and Silas are commissioned as representatives who will be sent to deliver the message to Antioch and other Christian communities.

Reflect: What role does the Holy Spirit play in resolving this issue?

Pray: Ask for the Holy Spirit's guidance at times of conflict resolution with others at home, in the workplace, or in your local church community.

Act: "Farewell" is not simply a word that ends a message but can also signify an instruction to continue to do well in one's life. Right now, what specific change do I need to make in my life in order to do well? How ready am I to make that change?

19i It is my judgment, therefore, that we ought to stop troubling the Gentiles who turn to God, 20j but tell them by letter to avoid pollution from idols, unlawful marriage, the meat of strangled animals, and blood. 21 For Moses, for generations now, has had those who proclaim him in every town, as he has been read in the synagogues every sabbath."

Letter of the Apostles.

22 Then the apostles and presbyters, in agreement with the whole church, decided to choose representatives and to send them to Antioch with Paul and Barnabas. The ones chosen were Judas, who was called Barsabbas, and Silas, leaders among the brothers. 23 This is the letter delivered by them: "The apostles and the presbyters, your brothers, to the brothers in Antioch, Syria, and Cilicia of Gentile origin: greetings. 24 Since we have heard that some of our number [who went out] without any mandate from us have upset you with their teachings and disturbed your peace of mind, 25 we have with one accord decided to choose representatives and to send them to you along with our beloved Barnabas and Paul, 26 who have dedicated their lives to the name of our Lord Jesus Christ. 27 So we are sending Judas and Silas who will also convey this same message by word of mouth: 28k 'It is the decision of the holy Spirit and of us not to place on you any burden beyond these necessities, 29l namely, to abstain from meat sacrificed to idols, from blood, from meats of strangled animals, and from unlawful marriage. If you keep free of these, you will be doing what is right. Farewell.'"

Delegates at Antioch.

30 And so they were sent on their journey. Upon their arrival in Antioch they called the assembly together and delivered the letter. 31 When the people read it, they were delighted with the exhortation. 32 Judas and Silas, who were themselves prophets, exhorted and strengthened the brothers with many words. 33 After they had spent some time there, they were sent off with greetings of peace from the brothers to those who had commissioned them. 34 * 35 But Paul and Barnabas remained in Antioch, teaching and proclaiming with many others the word of the Lord.

i. [15:19–20] 15:28–29; 21:25.
j. [15:20] Gn 9:4; Lv 3:17; 17:10–14.
k. [15:28–29] 15:19–20.
l. [15:29] Gn 9:4; Lv 3:17; 17:10–14.

/: THE MISSION OF PAUL TO THE ENDS OF THE EARTH

Read Acts 15:36–41

A dispute between Paul and Barnabas over John/Mark results in a parting of the ways.

Reflect: Two teams of missionaries emerge: Paul and Silas, Barnabas and John/Mark. Why does Luke describe dissension between the early church leaders? What does this say about human nature?

Pray: As this section notes, God works through human misunderstandings and disagreements. Seek God's guidance during times of personal disputes and misunderstandings.

Act: Human pride often affects our relationships with others. Misunderstandings arise, relationships are broken, and hurts may fester for a long time. Life is short; make an attempt to reconcile with a relative or person with whom you have had a misunderstanding.

Read Acts 16:1–10

In Lystra, Paul gets Timothy to accompany the missionaries as they begin their journey through Asia Minor and move westward.

Reflect: Timothy is recommended by those who knew him in Lystra and Iconium. Why is important to speak well of others?

Pray: In a vision, Paul hears words asking him to travel to Macedonia and to help those seeking his assistance there. Pray that, like Paul, you too may be willing to be open to meet new people in unfamiliar places.

Act: When the opportunity presents itself, speak well of another person.

Paul and Barnabas Separate.

36* After some time, Paul said to Barnabas, "Come, let us make a return visit to see how the brothers are getting on in all the cities where we proclaimed the word of the Lord." **37** Barnabas wanted to take with them also John, who was called Mark, **38m** but Paul insisted that they should not take with them someone who had deserted them at Pamphylia and who had not continued with them in their work. **39** So sharp was their disagreement that they separated. Barnabas took Mark and sailed to Cyprus. **40** But Paul chose Silas and departed after being commended by the brothers to the grace of the Lord. **41** He traveled through Syria and Cilicia bringing strength to the churches.

Paul in Lycaonia: Timothy.

16 **1a** He reached [also] Derbe and Lystra where there was a disciple named Timothy, the son of a Jewish woman who was a believer, but his father was a Greek. **2b** The brothers in Lystra and Iconium spoke highly of him, **3** and Paul wanted him to come along with him. On account of the Jews of that region, Paul had him circumcised,* for they all knew that his father was a Greek. **4** As they traveled from city to city, they handed on to the people for observance the decisions reached by the apostles and presbyters in Jerusalem. **5** Day after day the churches grew stronger in faith and increased in number.

Through Asia Minor.

6 They traveled through the Phrygian and Galatian territory because they had been prevented by the holy Spirit from preaching the message in the province of Asia. **7** When they came to Mysia, they tried to go on into Bithynia, but the Spirit of Jesus* did not allow them, **8** so they crossed through Mysia and came down to Troas. **9** During [the] night Paul had a vision. A Macedonian stood before him and implored him with these words, "Come over to Macedonia and help us." **10** When he had seen the vision, we* sought passage to Macedonia at once, concluding that God had called us to proclaim the good news to them.

Into Europe.

11 *We set sail from Troas, making a straight run for Samothrace, and on the next day to Neapolis, **12** and from there to Philippi, a leading city in that district of Macedonia and a Roman colony. We spent some time in

n. [15:38] 13:13.

. [16:1] 1Tm 1:2; 2Tm 1:5.
. [16:2] Phil 2:20.

Read Acts 16:11–40

The second missionary journey continues to Philippi, where Lydia and her household are baptized, an evil spirit is cast out of a fortune-teller, and, as a result, Paul and Silas are imprisoned. God sets them free from prison, and the jailer and his family are converted to the faith.

Reflect: Compare this release-from-prison scene of Paul and Silas with that of Peter, which was described in Acts 12:6–18.

Pray: Remember to pray for those who are in prison, whether for just or unjust causes.

Act: Both Lydia and the jailer extend hospitality to the missionaries. To whom should I be open to extending hospitality?

that city. 13 On the sabbath we went outside the city gate along the river where we thought there would be a place of prayer. We sat and spoke with the women who had gathered there. 14 One of them, a woman named Lydia, a dealer in purple cloth, from the city of Thyatira, a worshiper of God,* listened, and the Lord opened her heart to pay attention to what Paul was saying. 15 After she and her household had been baptized, she offered us an invitation, "If you consider me a believer in the Lord, come and stay at my home," and she prevailed on us.

Imprisonment at Philippi.

16 As we were going to the place of prayer, we met a slave girl with an oracular spirit,* who used to bring a large profit to her owners through her fortune-telling. 17 She began to follow Paul and us, shouting, "These people are slaves of the Most High God, who proclaim to you a way of salvation." 18 She did this for many days. Paul became annoyed, turned, and said to the spirit, "I command you in the name of Jesus Christ to come out of her." Then it came out at that moment.

19 When her owners saw that their hope of profit was gone, they seized Paul and Silas and dragged them to the public square before the local authorities. 20 They brought them before the magistrates* and said, "These people are Jews and are disturbing our city 21 and are advocating customs that are not lawful for us Romans to adopt or practice." 22c The crowd joined in the attack on them, and the magistrates had them stripped and ordered them to be beaten with rods. 23 After inflicting many blows on them, they threw them into prison and instructed the jailer to guard them securely. 24 When he received these instructions he put them in the innermost cell and secured their feet to a stake.

Deliverance from Prison.

25 About midnight, while Paul and Silas were praying and singing hymns to God as the prisoners listened, 26 there was suddenly such a severe earthquake that the foundations of the jail shook; all the doors flew open, and the chains of all were pulled loose. 27 When the jailer woke up and saw the prison doors wide open, he drew [his] sword and was about to kill himself, thinking that the prisoners had escaped. 28 But Paul shouted out in a loud voice, "Do no harm to yourself; we are all here." 29 He asked for a light and rushed in and, trembling with fear, he fell down before Paul and Silas. 30 Then he brought them out and said, "Sirs, what must I do to be saved?" 31 And they said, "Believe in the Lord

c. [16:22–23] 2Cor 11:25; Phil 1:30; 1Thes 2:2.

Jesus and you and your household will be saved." ³²So they spoke the word of the Lord to him and to everyone in his house. ³³He took them in at that hour of the night and bathed their wounds; then he and all his family were baptized at once. ³⁴He brought them up into his house and provided a meal and with his household rejoiced at having come to faith in God.

³⁵But when it was day, the magistrates sent the lictors* with the order, "Release those men." ³⁶The jailer reported the[se] words to Paul, "The magistrates have sent orders that you be released. Now, then, come out and go in peace." ³⁷ᵈBut Paul said to them, "They have beaten us publicly, even though we are Roman citizens and have not been tried, and have thrown us into prison. And now, are they going to release us secretly? By no means. Let them come themselves and lead us out."* ³⁸ᵉThe lictors reported these words to the magistrates, and they became alarmed when they heard that they were Roman citizens. ³⁹So they came and placated them, and led them out and asked that they leave the city. ⁴⁰When they had come out of the prison, they went to Lydia's house where they saw and encouraged the brothers, and then they left.

Read Acts 17:1–15

The mixed responses to the missionary proclamation continue in the journeys to Thessalonica and Beroea. Antagonism toward Paul and Silas escalates, crowds are stirred up, and the missionaries need to depart.

Reflect: What are some religious issues that cause commotion and rile people up?

Pray: Pray for those who are persecuted and experience ostracism because of their religious beliefs.

Act: Be willing take a stand on an issue that, while it may be unpopular, you know to be right.

Paul in Thessalonica.

17 ¹ᵃWhen they took the road through Amphipolis and Apollonia, they reached Thessalonica, where there was a synagogue of the Jews. ²Following his usual custom, Paul joined them, and for three sabbaths he entered into discussions with them from the scriptures, ³ᵇexpounding and demonstrating that the Messiah had to suffer and rise from the dead, and that "This is the Messiah, Jesus, whom I proclaim to you." ⁴Some of them were convinced and joined Paul and Silas; so, too, a great number of Greeks who were worshipers, and not a few of the prominent women. ⁵ᶜBut the Jews became jealous and recruited some worthless men loitering in the public square, formed a mob, and set the city in turmoil. They marched on the house of Jason, intending to bring them before the people's assembly. ⁶*When they could not find them, they dragged Jason and some of the brothers before the city magistrates, shouting, "These people who have been creating a disturbance all over the world have now come here, ⁷ᵈand Jason has welcomed them. They all act in opposition to the decrees of Caesar and claim instead that there is another king, Jesus."* ⁸They stirred up the crowd and the city magistrates who, upon hearing these charges, ⁹took a surety payment from Jason and the others before releasing them.

Paul in Beroea.

¹⁰The brothers immediately sent Paul and Silas to Beroea during the night. Upon arrival they went to the synagogue of the Jews. ¹¹ᵉThese Jews were more fairminded than those in Thessalonica, for they received the word with all willingness and examined the scriptures daily to determine whether these things were so.

. [16:37] 22:25.
. [16:38] 22:29.
. [17:1] 1Thes 2:1–2.
. [17:3] 3:18; Lk 24:25–26, 46.
. [17:5] Rom 16:21.
. [17:7] Lk 23:2; Jn 19:12–15.
. [17:11] Jn 5:39.

Read Acts 17:16–34

In Athens, Paul speaks to Jews in the synagogue and to Gentiles in the marketplace. Paul's speech at the Areopagus, the academic meeting place in Athens, makes an appeal to faith based not on scripture or religious beliefs but on philosophy and human reason.

Reflect: How does the Areopagus speech exemplify Paul's appeal to natural reason and ordinary human experience?

Pray: Religious faith and human reason are not competitors but rather complement each other. Pray for a deepened sense of faith that seeks better human understanding.

Act: In what specific ways do I promote dialogue and understanding between the sacred and the secular?

---

12 Many of them became believers, as did not a few of the influential Greek women and men. 13 But when the Jews of Thessalonica learned that the word of God had now been proclaimed by Paul in Beroea also, they came there too to cause a commotion and stir up the crowds. 14f So the brothers at once sent Paul on his way to the seacoast, while Silas and Timothy remained behind. 15 After Paul's escorts had taken him to Athens, they came away with instructions for Silas and Timothy to join him as soon as possible.

Paul in Athens.

16 *While Paul was waiting for them in Athens, he grew exasperated at the sight of the city full of idols. 17 So he debated in the synagogue with the Jews and with the worshipers, and daily in the public square with whoever happened to be there. 18 Even some of the Epicurean and Stoic philosophers* engaged him in discussion. Some asked, "What is this scavenger trying to say?" Others said, "He sounds like a promoter of foreign deities," because he was preaching about 'Jesus' and 'Resurrection.' 19g They took him and led him to the Areopagus* and said, "May we learn what this new teaching is that you speak of? 20 For you bring some strange notions to our ears; we should like to know what these things mean." 21 Now all the Athenians as well as the foreigners residing there used their time for nothing else but telling or hearing something new.

Paul's Speech at the Areopagus.

22 Then Paul stood up at the Areopagus and said: "You Athenians, I see that in every respect you are very religious. 23 For as I walked around looking carefully at your shrines, I even discovered an altar inscribed, 'To an Unknown God.'* What therefore you unknowingly worship, I proclaim to you. 24h The God who made the world and all that is in it, the Lord of heaven and earth, does not dwell in sanctuaries made by human hands, 25 nor is he served by human hands because he needs anything. Rather it is he who gives to everyone life and breath and everything. 26 He made from one* the whole human race to dwell on the entire surface of the earth, and he fixed the ordered seasons and the boundaries of their regions, 27i so that people might seek God, even perhaps grope for him and find him, though indeed he is not far from any one of us. 28 For 'In him we live and move and have our being,'* as even some of your poets have said, 'For we too are his offspring.' 29j Since therefore we are the offspring of God, we ought not to think that the divinity is like an image fashioned from gold, silver, or stone by human art and imagination. 30 God

---

f. [17:14] 1Thes 3:1–2.
g. [17:19] 1Cor 1:22.
h. [17:24] 7:48–50; Gn 1:1; 1Kgs 8:27; Is 42:5.
i. [17:27] Jer 23:23; Wis 13:6; Rom 1:19.
j. [17:29] 19:26; Is 40:18–20; 44:10–17; Rom 1:22–23.

has overlooked the times of ignorance, but now he demands that all people everywhere repent **31k** because he has established a day on which he will 'judge the world with justice' through a man he has appointed, and he has provided confirmation for all by raising him from the dead."

32 When they heard about resurrection of the dead, some began to scoff, but others said, "We should like to hear you on this some other time." **33** And so Paul left them. **34** But some did join him, and became believers. Among them were Dionysius, a member of the Court of the Areopagus, a woman named Damaris, and others with them.

Paul in Corinth.

18 **1** After this he left Athens and went to Corinth. **2a** There he met a Jew named Aquila, a native of Pontus, who had recently come from Italy with his wife Priscilla* because Claudius had ordered all the Jews to leave Rome. He went to visit them **3** and, because he practiced the same trade, stayed with them and worked, for they were tentmakers by trade. **4** Every sabbath, he entered into discussions in the synagogue, attempting to convince both Jews and Greeks.

5 When Silas and Timothy came down from Macedonia, Paul began to occupy himself totally with preaching the word, testifying to the Jews that the Messiah was Jesus. **6b** When they opposed him and reviled him, he shook out his garments* and said to them, "Your blood be on your heads! I am clear of responsibility. From now on I will go to the Gentiles." **7c** So he left there and went to a house belonging to a man named Titus Justus, a worshiper of God;* his house was next to a synagogue. **8d** Crispus,* the synagogue official, came to believe in the Lord along with his entire household, and many of the Corinthians who heard believed and were baptized. **9e** One night in a vision the Lord said to Paul, "Do not be afraid. Go on speaking, and do not be silent, **10** for I am with you. No one will attack and harm you, for I have many people in this city." **11** He settled there for a year and a half and taught the word of God among them.

Accusations before Gallio.

12 But when Gallio was proconsul of Achaia,* the Jews rose up together against Paul and brought him to the tribunal, **13** saying, "This man is inducing people to worship God contrary to the law."* **14** When Paul was about to reply, Gallio spoke to the Jews, "If it were a matter of some crime or malicious fraud, I should with reason hear the complaint of you Jews; **15** but since it is

. [17:31] 10:42.
a. [18:2] Rom 16:3.
b. [18:6] 13:51; Mt 10:14; 27:24–25; Mk 6:11; Lk 9:5; 10:10–11.
. [18:7] 13:46–47; 28:28.
. [18:8] 1Cor 1:14.
. [18:9–10] Jer 1:8.

a question of arguments over doctrine and titles an your own law, see to it yourselves. I do not wish to be judge of such matters." **16** And he drove them awa from the tribunal. **17** They all seized Sosthenes, the syn agogue official, and beat him in full view of the tribuna But none of this was of concern to Gallio.

Return to Syrian Antioch.

18f Paul remained for quite some time, and after say ing farewell to the brothers he sailed for Syria, togethe with Priscilla and Aquila. At Cenchreae he had his ha cut because he had taken a vow.* **19** When they reache Ephesus, he left them there, while he entered the syna gogue and held discussions with the Jews. **20** Althoug they asked him to stay for a longer time, he did not con sent, **21** but as he said farewell he promised, "I sha come back to you again, God willing." Then he set sa from Ephesus. **22** Upon landing at Caesarea, he went u and greeted the church* and then went down to Anti och. **23*** After staying there some time, he left and trav eled in orderly sequence through the Galatian countr and Phrygia, bringing strength to all the disciples.

Apollos.

24g A Jew named Apollos, a native of Alexandria, a eloquent speaker, arrived in Ephesus. He was an au thority on the scriptures.* **25** He had been instructed i the Way of the Lord and, with ardent spirit, spoke an taught accurately about Jesus, although he knew onl the baptism of John. **26** He began to speak boldly in th synagogue; but when Priscilla and Aquila heard him they took him aside and explained to him the Way [o God]* more accurately. **27** And when he wanted to cros to Achaia, the brothers encouraged him and wrote t the disciples there to welcome him. After his arrival h gave great assistance to those who had come to believ through grace. **28** He vigorously refuted the Jews in pub lic, establishing from the scriptures that the Messiah Jesus.

Paul in Ephesus.

19 **1*** While Apollos was in Corinth, Paul travele through the interior of the country and cam [down] to Ephesus where he found some disciples. **2** H said to them, "Did you receive the holy Spirit when yo became believers?" They answered him, "We have nev er even heard that there is a holy Spirit." **3** He said, "Hov were you baptized?" They replied, "With the baptism o John." **4a** Paul then said, "John baptized with a baptism of repentance, telling the people to believe in the on

f. [18:18] 21:24; Nm 6:18.
g. [18:24] 1Cor 1:12.

a. [19:4] 1:5; 11:16; 13:24–25; Mt 3:11; Mk 1:8; Lk 3:16.

Read Acts 19:8–22

Paul works signs and wonders, and a group of itinerant Jewish exorcists also want a share in his healing power.

Reflect: How do the extraordinary healing signs that Paul performs in this section compare with those of Peter described in Acts 5:12–16?

Pray: Pray for those who wish to renounce their former way of life and make a new beginning as Christians.

Act: This passage describes individuals who formerly practiced magic, rid themselves of their books, and burned them. Are there items that, because they lead you away from practicing your faith, you should dispose of?

who was to come after him, that is, in Jesus." 5 When they heard this, they were baptized in the name of the Lord Jesus. 6b And when Paul laid [his] hands on them, the holy Spirit came upon them, and they spoke in tongues and prophesied. 7 Altogether there were about twelve men.

8 He entered the synagogue, and for three months debated boldly with persuasive arguments about the kingdom of God. 9 But when some in their obstinacy and disbelief disparaged the Way before the assembly, he withdrew and took his disciples with him and began to hold daily discussions in the lecture hall of Tyrannus. 10 This continued for two years with the result that all the inhabitants of the province of Asia heard the word of the Lord, Jews and Greeks alike. 11 So extraordinary were the mighty deeds God accomplished at the hands of Paul 12c that when face cloths or aprons that touched his skin were applied to the sick, their diseases left them and the evil spirits came out of them.

The Jewish Exorcists.

13 Then some itinerant Jewish exorcists tried to invoke the name of the Lord Jesus over those with evil spirits, saying, "I adjure you by the Jesus whom Paul preaches." 14 When the seven sons of Sceva, a Jewish high priest, tried to do this, 15 the evil spirit said to them in reply, "Jesus I recognize, Paul I know, but who are you?" 16 The person with the evil spirit then sprang at them and subdued them all. He so overpowered them that they fled naked and wounded from that house. 17 When this became known to all the Jews and Greeks who lived in Ephesus, fear fell upon them all, and the name of the Lord Jesus was held in great esteem. 18 Many of those who had become believers came forward and openly acknowledged their former practices. 19 Moreover, a large number of those who had practiced magic collected their books and burned them in public. They calculated their value and found it to be fifty thousand silver pieces. 20 Thus did the word of the Lord continue to spread with influence and power.

Paul's Plans.

21d When this was concluded, Paul made up his mind to travel through Macedonia and Achaia, and then to go on to Jerusalem, saying, "After I have been there, I must visit Rome also." 22 Then he sent to Macedonia two of his assistants, Timothy and Erastus, while he himself stayed for a while in the province of Asia.

The Riot of the Silversmiths.

23 About that time a serious disturbance broke out

. [19:6] 8:15–17; 10:44, 46.
. [19:12] 5:15–16; Lk 8:44–47.
. [19:21] 23:11; Rom 1:13; 15:22–32.

Read Acts 19:23–40

Paul's successful preaching has an adverse effect on the commerce and trade of the silversmiths who make statues of the goddess Artemis. As a result, a riot occurs at the theater in Ephesus.

Reflect: What happens when religious conversion affects industry and business?

Pray: Business, commerce, and trade should be about more than simply the bottom line of making huge profits and generating successful sales. Pray for justice in the workplace, respect for the dignity and economic well-being of the laborer, and the development of an economic system geared to the improvement of society and the human condition.

Act: In deciding to make a purchase, consider not simply price but also fair business practices as well as justice for the individuals who produce the item.

concerning the Way. 24 There was a silversmith name Demetrius who made miniature silver shrines c Artemis* and provided no little work for the craftsmen 25 He called a meeting of these and other workers in re lated crafts and said, "Men, you know well that ou prosperity derives from this work. 26e As you can now see and hear, not only in Ephesus but throughout mos of the province of Asia this Paul has persuaded an misled a great number of people by saying that god made by hands are not gods at all. 27 The danger grows not only that our business will be discredited, but als that the temple of the great goddess Artemis will be c no account, and that she whom the whole province c Asia and all the world worship will be stripped of he magnificence."

28 When they heard this, they were filled with fur and began to shout, "Great is Artemis of the Eph esians!" 29f The city was filled with confusion, and th people rushed with one accord into the theater, seizin Gaius and Aristarchus, the Macedonians, Paul's trave ing companions. 30 Paul wanted to go before the crowc but the disciples would not let him, 31 and even some c the Asiarchs* who were friends of his sent word to hin advising him not to venture into the theater. 32 Mean while, some were shouting one thing, others somethin else; the assembly was in chaos, and most of the peo ple had no idea why they had come together. 33 Som of the crowd prompted Alexander, as the Jews pushe him forward, and Alexander signaled with his hand tha he wished to explain something to the gathering. 34 Bu when they recognized that he was a Jew, they all shout ed in unison, for about two hours, "Great is Artemis c the Ephesians!" 35 Finally the town clerk restrained th crowd and said, "You Ephesians, what person is ther who does not know that the city of the Ephesians is th guardian of the temple* of the great Artemis and of he image that fell from the sky? 36 Since these things ar undeniable, you must calm yourselves and not do any thing rash. 37 The men you brought here are not templ robbers, nor have they insulted our goddess. 38 If Deme trius and his fellow craftsmen have a complaint agains anyone, courts are in session, and there are proconsuls Let them bring charges against one another. 39 If yo have anything further to investigate, let the matter b settled in the lawful assembly, 40 for, as it is, we are i danger of being charged with rioting because of today' conduct. There is no cause for it. We shall [not]* be abl to give a reason for this demonstration." With thes words he dismissed the assembly.

e. [19:26] 17:29.
f. [19:29] Col 4:10.

Read Acts 20:1–12

Paul leaves Ephesus and moves on to Macedonia and Greece. He encourages and strengthens the communities already established. Others accompany him. A humorous account of the effect that Paul's lengthy preaching has upon a young man named Eutychus is described.

Reflect: People accompany Paul on his missionary journeys. Why is this important for the Christian communities?

Pray: Pray for travelers, that they may have a safe journey.

Act: Paul's speaking at such great length caused Eutychus to fall asleep. When you are talking, be careful not to dominate the conversation or go on endlessly.

Journey to Macedonia and Greece.

20 ^{1a} When the disturbance was over, Paul had the disciples summoned and, after encouraging them, he bade them farewell and set out on his journey to Macedonia. ² As he traveled throughout those regions, he provided many words of encouragement for them. Then he arrived in Greece, ³ where he stayed for three months. But when a plot was made against him by the Jews as he was about to set sail for Syria, he decided to return by way of Macedonia.

Return to Troas.

^{4b} Sopater, the son of Pyrrhus, from Beroea, accompanied him, as did Aristarchus and Secundus from Thessalonica, Gaius from Derbe, Timothy, and Tychicus and Trophimus from Asia ^{5c} who went on ahead and waited for us* at Troas. ⁶ We sailed from Philippi after the feast of Unleavened Bread,* and rejoined them five days later in Troas, where we spent a week.

Eutychus Restored to Life.

⁷ On the first day of the week* when we gathered to break bread, Paul spoke to them because he was going to leave on the next day, and he kept on speaking until midnight. ⁸ There were many lamps in the upstairs room where we were gathered, ⁹ and a young man named Eutychus who was sitting on the window sill was sinking into a deep sleep as Paul talked on and on. Once overcome by sleep, he fell down from the third story and when he was picked up, he was dead. ^{10d} Paul went down,* threw himself upon him, and said as he embraced him, "Don't be alarmed; there is life in him." ¹¹ Then he returned upstairs, broke the bread, and ate; after a long conversation that lasted until daybreak, he departed. ¹² And they took the boy away alive and were immeasurably comforted.

Journey to Miletus.

¹³ We went ahead to the ship and set sail for Assos where we were to take Paul on board, as he had arranged, since he was going overland. ¹⁴ When he met us in Assos, we took him aboard and went on to Mitylene. ¹⁵ We sailed away from there on the next day and reached a point off Chios, and a day later we reached Samos, and on the following day we arrived at Miletus. ^{16*} Paul had decided to sail past Ephesus in order not to lose time in the province of Asia, for he was hurrying to be in Jerusalem, if at all possible, for the day of Pentecost.

[20:1] 1Cor 16:1.
[20:4] Rom 16:21.
[20:5] 21:29; 2Tm 4:20.
[20:10] 1Kgs 17:17–24; 2Kgs 4:30–37;
Mt 9:24; Mk 5:39; Lk 8:52.

Read Acts 20:13–38

Paul travels to Miletus and offers an emotional farewell speech to the church leaders of Ephesus.

Reflect: What are the major aspects and components of Paul's farewell speech? Compare his words with those of Jesus' farewell discourse in Luke 22:14–37. Notice the similarities.

Pray: Saying good-bye to others is never easy. In your prayer, remember with gratitude those who have played an important role in your life.

Act: When people who have shared caring and understanding move on in their lives (because of retirement, relocation, change in work, school commencements, etc.), express appreciation and gratitude for the positive influence they have had on your life.

Paul's Farewell Speech at Miletus.

17 From Miletus he had the presbyters of the churcl at Ephesus summoned. **18** When they came to him, h addressed them, "You know how I lived among you th whole time from the day I first came to the province c Asia. **19** I served the Lord with all humility and with th tears and trials that came to me because of the plots c the Jews, **20** and I did not at all shrink from telling yo what was for your benefit, or from teaching you in pub lic or in your homes. **21** I earnestly bore witness for botl Jews and Greeks to repentance before God and to faitl in our Lord Jesus. **22** But now, compelled by the Spirit, am going to Jerusalem. What will happen to me there do not know, **23e** except that in one city after another th holy Spirit has been warning me that imprisonment an hardships await me. **24f** Yet I consider life of no impor tance to me, if only I may finish my course and the min istry that I received from the Lord Jesus, to bear witnes to the gospel of God's grace.

25 "But now I know that none of you to whom preached the kingdom during my travels will ever se my face again. **26** And so I solemnly declare to you thi day that I am not responsible for the blood of any c you, **27** for I did not shrink from proclaiming to you th entire plan of God. **28g** Keep watch over yourselves an over the whole flock of which the holy Spirit has ap pointed you overseers,* in which you tend the churcl of God that he acquired with his own blood. **29h** I knov that after my departure savage wolves will com among you, and they will not spare the flock. **30i** An from your own group, men will come forward pervert ing the truth to draw the disciples away after them. **3** So be vigilant and remember that for three years, nigl and day, I unceasingly admonished each of you witl tears. **32** And now I commend you to God and to tha gracious word of his that can build you up and give yo the inheritance among all who are consecrated. **33** have never wanted anyone's silver or gold or clothing **34k** You know well that these very hands have serve my needs and my companions. **35l** In every way I hav shown you that by hard work of that sort we must hel the weak, and keep in mind the words of the Lord Je sus who himself said, 'It is more blessed to give than t receive.'"

36 When he had finished speaking he knelt down an prayed with them all. **37** They were all weeping loudly a they threw their arms around Paul and kissed him, **38** fo they were deeply distressed that he had said that the would never see his face again. Then they escorted hin to the ship.

e. [20:23] 9:16.
f. [20:24] 2Tm 4:7.
g. [20:28] Jn 21:15–17; 1Pt 5:2.
h. [20:29] Jn 10:12.
i. [20:30] Mt 7:15; 2 Pt 2:1–3; 1Jn 2:18–19.
j. [20:31] 1Thes 2:11.
k. [20:34] 1Cor 4:12; 1Thes 2:9; 2Thes 3:8.
l. [20:35] Sir 4:31.

Arrival at Tyre.

Read Acts 21:1–14

Paul continues traveling by sea to various locations. Agabus, the Jewish Christian prophet previously mentioned in Acts 11:28, performs a dramatic sign with Paul's belt by binding his own hands and feet.

Reflect: What other Bible stories describe this action of binding? Compare Agabus's actions and their meaning with those in Jeremiah 27:1–15 and John 21:15–19.

Pray: There will be times in our lives when we may feel bound and called to go in a different direction from where we would like to go. These are occasions to pray and ask for God's strength.

Act: A Christian disciple who prays the Lord's Prayer should live by the same words that Paul spoke: "The Lord's will be done."

21 ¹ *When we had taken leave of them we set sail, made a straight run for Cos, and on the next day for Rhodes, and from there to Patara. ² Finding a ship crossing to Phoenicia, we went on board and put out to sea. ³ We caught sight of Cyprus but passed by it on our left and sailed on toward Syria and put in at Tyre where the ship was to unload cargo. ⁴ There we sought out the disciples and stayed for a week. They kept telling Paul through the Spirit not to embark for Jerusalem. ⁵ At the end of our stay we left and resumed our journey. All of them, women and children included, escorted us out of the city, and after kneeling on the beach to pray, ⁶ we bade farewell to one another. Then we boarded the ship, and they returned home.

Arrival at Ptolemais and Caesarea.

⁷ We continued the voyage and came from Tyre to Ptolemais, where we greeted the brothers and stayed a day with them. ⁸ᵃ On the next day we resumed the trip and came to Caesarea, where we went to the house of Philip the evangelist, who was one of the Seven,* and stayed with him. ⁹ He had four virgin daughters gifted with prophecy. ¹⁰ We had been there several days when a prophet named Agabus* came down from Judea. ¹¹ᵇ He came up to us, took Paul's belt, bound his own feet and hands with it, and said, "Thus says the holy Spirit: This is the way the Jews will bind the owner of this belt in Jerusalem, and they will hand him over to the Gentiles."* ¹² When we heard this, we and the local residents begged him not to go up to Jerusalem. ¹³ᶜ Then Paul replied, "What are you doing, weeping and breaking my heart? I am prepared not only to be bound but even to die in Jerusalem for the name of the Lord Jesus." ¹⁴ᵈ Since he would not be dissuaded we let the matter rest, saying, "The Lord's will be done."*

Paul and James in Jerusalem.

¹⁵ After these days we made preparations for our journey, then went up to Jerusalem. ¹⁶ Some of the disciples from Caesarea came along to lead us to the house of Mnason, a Cypriot, a disciple of long standing, with whom we were to stay. ¹⁷* When we reached Jerusalem the brothers welcomed us warmly. ¹⁸ The next day, Paul accompanied us on a visit to James, and all the presbyters were present. ¹⁹ He greeted them, then proceeded to tell them in detail what God had accomplished among the Gentiles through his ministry. ²⁰ They praised God when they heard it but said to him, "Brother, you see how many thousands of believers there are from among the Jews, and they are all zeal-

ous observers of the law. 21 They have been informed that you are teaching all the Jews who live among the Gentiles to abandon Moses and that you are telling them not to circumcise their children or to observe their customary practices. 22 What is to be done? They will surely hear that you have arrived. 23*e So do what we tell you. We have four men who have taken a vow. 24 Take these men and purify yourself with them, and pay their expenses* that they may have their heads shaved. In this way everyone will know that there is nothing to the reports they have been given about you but that you yourself live in observance of the law. 25f As for the Gentiles who have come to believe, we sent them our decision that they abstain from meat sacrificed to idols, from blood, from the meat of strangled animals, and from unlawful marriage."* 26g So Paul took the men, and on the next day after purifying himself together with them entered the temple to give notice of the day when the purification would be completed and the offering made for each of them.

Paul's Arrest.

27 When the seven days were nearly completed, the Jews from the province of Asia noticed him in the temple, stirred up the whole crowd, and laid hands on him, 28h shouting, "Fellow Israelites, help us. This is the man who is teaching everyone everywhere against the people and the law and this place, and what is more, he has even brought Greeks into the temple and defiled this sacred place."* 29 For they had previously seen Trophimus the Ephesian in the city with him and supposed that Paul had brought him into the temple. 30 The whole city was in turmoil with people rushing together. They seized Paul and dragged him out of the temple, and immediately the gates were closed. 31 While they were trying to kill him, a report reached the cohort commander* that all Jerusalem was rioting. 32 He immediately took soldiers and centurions and charged down on them. When they saw the commander and the soldiers they stopped beating Paul. 33 The cohort commander came forward, arrested him, and ordered him to be secured with two chains; he tried to find out who he might be and what he had done. 34 Some in the mob shouted one thing, others something else; so, since he was unable to ascertain the truth because of the uproar, he ordered Paul to be brought into the compound. 35 When he reached the steps, he was carried by the soldiers because of the violence of the mob, 36*i for a crowd of people followed and shouted, "Away with him!"

37 Just as Paul was about to be taken into the compound, he said to the cohort commander, "May I say

e. [21:23–27] 18:18; Nm 6:1–21.
f. [21:25] 15:19–20, 28–29.
g. [21:26] 1Cor 9:20.
h. [21:28] Rom 15:31.
i. [21:36] 22:22; Lk 23:18; Jn 19:15.

Read Acts 22:1–21

Paul speaks before the Jews in Jerusalem. He offers an autobiographical account of his conversion.

Reflect: Compare Paul's version of his conversion with what was previously narrated in Acts 9:1–30.

Pray: Part of Paul's conversion experience involved accepting assistance from Ananias. It is not always easy to allow others to help us. Pray for a sense of humility and the willingness to let others help you.

Act: Express appreciation to those who have helped you in your life. Do not take others for granted, and when people are helpful to you, make an effort to see them as God's instruments.

something to you?" He replied, "Do you speak Greek? **38j** So then you are not the Egyptian* who started a revolt some time ago and led the four thousand assassins into the desert?" **39** Paul answered, "I am a Jew, of Tarsus in Cilicia, a citizen of no mean city; I request you to permit me to speak to the people." **40** When he had given his permission, Paul stood on the steps and motioned with his hand to the people; and when all was quiet he addressed them in Hebrew.*

Paul's Defense before the Jerusalem Jews.

22 **1*** "My brothers and fathers, listen to what I am about to say to you in my defense." **2** When they heard him addressing them in Hebrew they became all the more quiet. And he continued, **3a** "I am a Jew, born in Tarsus in Cilicia, but brought up in this city. At the feet of Gamaliel I was educated strictly in our ancestral law and was zealous for God, just as all of you are today. **4b** I persecuted this Way to death, binding both men and women and delivering them to prison. **5** Even the high priest and the whole council of elders can testify on my behalf. For from them I even received letters to the brothers and set out for Damascus to bring back to Jerusalem in chains for punishment those there as well.

6c "On that journey as I drew near to Damascus, about noon a great light from the sky suddenly shone around me. **7d** I fell to the ground and heard a voice saying to me, 'Saul, Saul, why are you persecuting me?' **8e** I replied, 'Who are you, sir?' And he said to me, 'I am Jesus the Nazorean whom you are persecuting.' **9f** My companions saw the light but did not hear the voice of the one who spoke to me. **10g** I asked, 'What shall I do, sir?' The Lord answered me, 'Get up and go into Damascus, and there you will be told about everything appointed for you to do.' **11h** Since I could see nothing because of the brightness of that light, I was led by hand by my companions and entered Damascus.

12i "A certain Ananias, a devout observer of the law, and highly spoken of by all the Jews who lived there, **13** came to me and stood there and said, 'Saul, my brother, regain your sight.' And at that very moment I regained my sight and saw him. **14** Then he said, 'The God of our ancestors designated you to know his will, to see the Righteous One, and to hear the sound of his voice; **15** for you will be his witness* before all to what you have seen and heard. **16** Now, why delay? Get up and have yourself baptized and your sins washed away, calling upon his name.'

17 "After I had returned to Jerusalem and while I was praying in the temple, I fell into a trance **18** and saw the Lord saying to me, 'Hurry, leave Jerusalem at once, be-

[21:38] 5:36–37.

[22:3] 5:34; 26:4–5; 2Cor 11:22; Gal 1:13–14; Phil 3:5–6.
[22:4] 8:3; 9:1–2; 22:19; 26:9–11; Phil 3:6.
[22:6] 9:3; 26:13; 1Cor 15:8.
[22:7] 9:4; 26:14.
[22:8] 9:5; 26:15; Mt 25:40.
[22:9] 9:7; 26:13–14.
[22:10] 9:6; 26:16.
[22:11] 9:8.
[22:12–16] 9:10–19.

Read Acts 22:22—23:11

Paul is imprisoned and makes an appeal to be tried as a Roman citizen. He defends himself before the Sanhedrin and cleverly offers a viewpoint about the resurrection that results in a dispute between the Pharisees and the Sadducees.

Reflect: The words that the Lord speaks to Paul are also spoken to us: "Take courage" in bearing witness before others.

Pray: Bring before God in your prayers any present fears, troubles, or difficulties that you are facing and ask for courage in dealing with them.

Act: Take a few moments and repeat to yourself the words, "Take courage." See them as words of encouragement when dealing with the struggles of daily life, knowing and trusting that the Lord is there to help you.

cause they will not accept your testimony about me 19j But I replied, 'Lord, they themselves know that fror synagogue to synagogue I used to imprison and bea those who believed in you. 20k And when the blood c your witness Stephen was being shed, I myself stood b giving my approval and keeping guard over the cloak of his murderers.' 21l Then he said to me, 'Go, I sha send you far away to the Gentiles.'"*

Paul Imprisoned.

22m They listened to him until he said this, but the they raised their voices and shouted, "Take such a on as this away from the earth. It is not right that he shoul live."* 23 And as they were yelling and throwing off the cloaks and flinging dust into the air, 24 the cohort com mander ordered him to be brought into the compoun and gave instruction that he be interrogated under th lash to determine the reason why they were makin such an outcry against him. 25n But when they ha stretched him out for the whips, Paul said to the centu rion on duty, "Is it lawful for you to scourge a man wh is a Roman citizen and has not been tried?"* 26 When th centurion heard this, he went to the cohort commande and reported it, saying, "What are you going to do? Thi man is a Roman citizen." 27 Then the commander cam and said to him, "Tell me, are you a Roman citizen? "Yes," he answered. 28 The commander replied, "I ac quired this citizenship for a large sum of money." Pau said, "But I was born one." 29 At once those who wer going to interrogate him backed away from him, an the commander became alarmed when he realized tha he was a Roman citizen and that he had had him bound

Paul before the Sanhedrin.

30 The next day, wishing to determine the truth abou why he was being accused by the Jews, he freed hin and ordered the chief priests and the whole Sanhedri to convene. Then he brought Paul down and made hin stand before them.

23 1a Paul looked intently at the Sanhedrin and said "My brothers, I have conducted myself with perfectly clear conscience before God to this day." 2 Th high priest Ananias* ordered his attendants to strike hi mouth. 3b Then Paul said to him, "God will strike you, you whitewashed wall. Do you indeed sit in judgmen upon me according to the law and yet in violation of th law order me to be struck?" 4 The attendants said "Would you revile God's high priest?" 5c Paul answered "Brothers, I did not realize he was the high priest. For i is written, 'You shall not curse a ruler of your people.'"

j. [22:19] 8:3; 9:1–2; 22:4–5; 26:9–11.
k. [22:20] 7:58; 8:1.
l. [22:21] 9:15; Gal 2:7–9.
m. [22:22] 21:36; Lk 23:18; Jn 19:15.
n. [22:25] 16:37.

a. [23:1] 24:16.
b. [23:3] Ez 13:10–15; Mt 23:27.
c. [23:5] Ex 22:27.

⁶ᵈ Paul was aware that some were Sadducees and some Pharisees, so he called out before the Sanhedrin, "My brothers, I am a Pharisee, the son of Pharisees; [I] am on trial for hope in the resurrection of the dead." ⁷ When he said this, a dispute broke out between the Pharisees and Sadducees, and the group became divided. ⁸ᵉ For the Sadducees say that there is no resurrection or angels or spirits, while the Pharisees acknowledge all three. ⁹ A great uproar occurred, and some scribes belonging to the Pharisee party stood up and sharply argued, "We find nothing wrong with this man. Suppose a spirit or an angel has spoken to him?" ¹⁰ The dispute was so serious that the commander, afraid that Paul would be torn to pieces by them, ordered his troops to go down and rescue him from their midst and take him into the compound. ¹¹*ᶠ The following night the Lord stood by him and said, "Take courage. For just as you have borne witness to my cause in Jerusalem, so you must also bear witness in Rome."

Transfer to Caesarea.

¹² When day came, the Jews made a plot and bound themselves by oath not to eat or drink until they had killed Paul. ¹³ There were more than forty who formed this conspiracy. ¹⁴ They went to the chief priests and elders and said, "We have bound ourselves by a solemn oath to taste nothing until we have killed Paul. ¹⁵ You, together with the Sanhedrin, must now make an official request to the commander to have him bring him down to you, as though you meant to investigate his case more thoroughly. We on our part are prepared to kill him before he arrives." ¹⁶ The son of Paul's sister, however, heard about the ambush; so he went and entered the compound and reported it to Paul. ¹⁷ Paul then called one of the centurions* and requested, "Take this young man to the commander; he has something to report to him." ¹⁸ So he took him and brought him to the commander and explained, "The prisoner Paul called me and asked that I bring this young man to you; he has something to say to you." ¹⁹ The commander took him by the hand, drew him aside, and asked him privately, "What is it you have to report to me?" ²⁰ He replied, "The Jews have conspired to ask you to bring Paul down to the Sanhedrin tomorrow, as though they meant to inquire about him more thoroughly, ²¹ but do not believe them. More than forty of them are lying in wait for him; they have bound themselves by oath not to eat or drink until they have killed him. They are now ready and only wait for your consent." ²² As the commander dismissed the young man he directed him, "Tell no one that you gave me this information."

ₖ. [23:6] 24:15, 21; 26:5; Phil 3:5.
₂. [23:8] Mt 22:23; Lk 20:27.
  [23:11] 19:21.

Read Acts 24:1–23

Paul is placed on trial before the governor, Felix. During his defense, Paul describes Christianity as "the Way," which is based upon Jewish worship and tradition but also includes a distinctive belief in the resurrection.

Reflect: This section describes the procedures of how trials were conducted in the Roman Empire during the first century AD. Notice how both sides try to ingratiate themselves with the governor for a favorable hearing.

Pray: Apart from courtroom settings, one can experience trials before others. Pray for the Spirit's guidance and direction during times when you are called to testify on behalf of your Christian faith.

Act: In this story, both sides say kind words to the governor in order to win him over. Consider the importance of kindness the next time you are tempted to speak badly about another.

23 Then he summoned two of the centurions and said, "Get two hundred soldiers ready to go to Caesarea by nine o'clock tonight,* along with seventy horsemen and two hundred auxiliaries. **24** Provide mounts for Paul to ride and give him safe conduct to Felix the governor. **25** Then he wrote a letter with this content: **26*** "Claudius Lysias to his excellency the governor Felix, greetings. **27g** This man, seized by the Jews and about to be murdered by them, I rescued after intervening with my troops when I learned that he was a Roman citizen. **28** I wanted to learn the reason for their accusations against him so I brought him down to their Sanhedrin. **29h** I discovered that he was accused in matters of controversial questions of their law and not of any charge deserving death or imprisonment. **30** Since it was brought to my attention that there will be a plot against the man, I am sending him to you at once, and have also notified his accusers to state [their case] against him before you."

31 So the soldiers, according to their orders, took Paul and escorted him by night to Antipatris. **32** The next day they returned to the compound, leaving the horsemen to complete the journey with him. **33** When they arrived in Caesarea they delivered the letter to the governor and presented Paul to him. **34** When he had read it and asked to what province he belonged, and learned that he was from Cilicia, **35** he said, "I shall hear your case when your accusers arrive." Then he ordered that he be held in custody in Herod's praetorium.

Trial before Felix.

24 **1** Five days later the high priest Ananias came down with some elders and an advocate, a certain Tertullus, and they presented formal charges against Paul to the governor. **2** When he was called, Tertullus began to accuse him, saying, "Since we have attained much peace through you, and reforms have been accomplished in this nation through your provident care, **3** we acknowledge this in every way and everywhere, most excellent Felix, with all gratitude. **4** But in order not to detain you further, I ask you to give us a brief hearing with your customary graciousness. **5a** We found this man to be a pest; he creates dissension among Jews all over the world and is a ringleader of the sect of the Nazoreans.* **6b** He even tried to desecrate our temple, but we arrested him. **7 * 8** If you examine him you will be able to learn from him for yourself about everything of which we are accusing him." **9** The Jews also joined in the attack and asserted that these things were so.

10* Then the governor motioned to him to speak and Paul replied, "I know that you have been a judge over

g. [23:27] 21:30–34; 22:27.
h. [23:29] 18:14–15; 25:18–19.

a. [24:5] 24:14; Lk 23:2.
b. [24:6] 21:28.

Read Acts 24:24—25:12

Paul remains in captivity in Caesarea. Festus conducts the next trial and Paul makes the appeal as a Roman citizen to be tried by the emperor.

Reflect: Paul identifies himself as both a religious believer and a citizen of society. How are these identities related to each other?

Pray: Pray to be, like Paul, strong in your personal convictions.

Act: Keep aware and informed as a way of being a responsible citizen of society. Participate in political processes to enact just and fair laws.

this nation for many years and so I am pleased to make my defense before you. **11** As you can verify, not more than twelve days have passed since I went up to Jerusalem to worship. **12** Neither in the temple, nor in the synagogues, nor anywhere in the city did they find me arguing with anyone or instigating a riot among the people. **13** Nor can they prove to you the accusations they are now making against me. **14c** But this I do admit to you, that according to the Way, which they call a sect, I worship the God of our ancestors and I believe everything that is in accordance with the law and written in the prophets. **15d** I have the same hope in God as they themselves have that there will be a resurrection of the righteous and the unrighteous. **16e** Because of this, I always strive to keep my conscience clear before God and man. **17f** After many years, I came to bring alms for my nation and offerings. **18g** While I was so engaged, they found me, after my purification, in the temple without a crowd or disturbance. **19** But some Jews from the province of Asia, who should be here before you to make whatever accusation they might have against me—**20** or let these men themselves state what crime they discovered when I stood before the Sanhedrin, **21h** unless it was my one outcry as I stood among them, that 'I am on trial before you today for the resurrection of the dead.'"

22 Then Felix, who was accurately informed about the Way, postponed the trial, saying, "When Lysias the commander comes down, I shall decide your case." **23** He gave orders to the centurion that he should be kept in custody but have some liberty, and that he should not prevent any of his friends from caring for his needs.

Captivity in Caesarea.

24* Several days later Felix came with his wife Drusilla, who was Jewish. He had Paul summoned and listened to him speak about faith in Christ Jesus. **25** But as he spoke about righteousness and self-restraint and the coming judgment, Felix became frightened and said, "You may go for now; when I find an opportunity I shall summon you again." **26** At the same time he hoped that a bribe would be offered him by Paul, and so he sent for him very often and conversed with him.

27 Two years passed and Felix was succeeded by Porcius Festus. Wishing to ingratiate himself with the Jews, Felix left Paul in prison.*

Appeal to Caesar.

25 **1** Three days after his arrival in the province, Festus went up from Caesarea to Jerusalem

c. [24:14] 24:5.
d. [24:15] Dn 12:2; Jn 5:28–29.
e. [24:16] 23:1.
f. [24:17] Rom 15:25–26; Gal 2:10.
g. [24:18–19] 21:26–30.
h. [24:21] 23:6; 24:15.

Read Acts 25:13-27

Festus invites King Agrippa to hear Paul's case, explaining that the issue appears to be a type of internal religious dispute.

Reflect: How would you describe the motives of Festus? Personal interest? A concern for what is best for the individual? An attempt to please higher authority?

Pray: Pray for a legal system based on fairness and just laws, not motivated by corruption, political gain, or exploiting the less fortunate.

Act: Various levels of authority are involved in resolving disputes and conflicts. Follow the principle of subsidiarity and try to settle issues at the lowest level possible rather than appealing to higher authorities for resolution.

² where the chief priests and Jewish leaders presented him their formal charges against Paul.* They asked him ³ as a favor to have him sent to Jerusalem, for they were plotting to kill him along the way. ⁴ Festus replied that Paul was being held in custody in Caesarea and that he himself would be returning there shortly. ⁵ He said, "Let your authorities come down with me, and if this man has done something improper, let them accuse him."

⁶ After spending no more than eight or ten days with them, he went down to Caesarea, and on the following day took his seat on the tribunal and ordered that Paul be brought in. ⁷ When he appeared, the Jews who had come down from Jerusalem surrounded him and brought many serious charges against him, which they were unable to prove. ⁸ In defending himself Paul said, "I have committed no crime either against the Jewish law or against the temple or against Caesar." ⁹* Then Festus, wishing to ingratiate himself with the Jews, said to Paul in reply, "Are you willing to go up to Jerusalem and there stand trial before me on these charges?" ¹⁰ Paul answered, "I am standing before the tribunal of Caesar; this is where I should be tried. I have committed no crime against the Jews, as you very well know. ¹¹ If I have committed a crime or done anything deserving death, I do not seek to escape the death penalty; but if there is no substance to the charges they are bringing against me, then no one has the right to hand me over to them. I appeal to Caesar." ¹² Then Festus, after conferring with his council, replied, "You have appealed to Caesar. To Caesar you will go."

Paul before King Agrippa.

¹³ When a few days had passed, King Agrippa and Bernice* arrived in Caesarea on a visit to Festus. ¹⁴ᵃ Since they spent several days there, Festus referred Paul's case to the king, saying, "There is a man here left in custody by Felix. ¹⁵ When I was in Jerusalem the chief priests and the elders of the Jews brought charges against him and demanded his condemnation. ¹⁶ I answered them that it was not Roman practice to hand over an accused person before he has faced his accusers and had the opportunity to defend himself against their charge. ¹⁷ So when [they] came together here, I made no delay; the next day I took my seat on the tribunal and ordered the man to be brought in. ¹⁸ᵇ His accusers stood around him, but did not charge him with any of the crimes I suspected. ¹⁹ Instead they had some issues with him about their own religion and about a certain Jesus who had died but who Paul claimed was alive. ²⁰ Since I was at a loss how to investigate this controversy, I asked if he were willing to go to Jerusalem

a. [25:14] 24:27.
b. [25:18-19] 18:14-15; 23:29.

Read Acts 26:1–23

Paul gives his testimony before King Agrippa. Paul's discourse is offered from both a theological and a personal perspective as he gives witness before a king and a governor. Paul's conversion is described for a third time (previously in Acts 9 and 22).

Reflect: Notice how Paul provides a summary of his life and missionary activity.

Pray: Ask that, like Paul, you too may recognize the presence of God in your life.

Act: Take a few moments to consider how your understanding of God and of the ways in which God has acted in your life has changed over the years. What have you learned?

and there stand trial on these charges. **21** And when Paul appealed that he be held in custody for the Emperor's decision, I ordered him held until I could send him to Caesar." **22** Agrippa said to Festus, "I too should like to hear this man." He replied, "Tomorrow you will hear him."

23 The next day Agrippa and Bernice came with great ceremony and entered the audience hall in the company of cohort commanders and the prominent men of the city and, by command of Festus, Paul was brought in. **24** And Festus said, "King Agrippa and all you here present with us, look at this man about whom the whole Jewish populace petitioned me here and in Jerusalem, clamoring that he should live no longer. **25** I found, however, that he had done nothing deserving death, and so when he appealed to the Emperor, I decided to send him. **26** But I have nothing definite to write about him to our sovereign; therefore I have brought him before all of you, and particularly before you, King Agrippa, so that I may have something to write as a result of this investigation. **27** For it seems senseless to me to send up a prisoner without indicating the charges against him."

King Agrippa Hears Paul.

26 **1** Then Agrippa said to Paul, "You may now speak on your own behalf." So Paul stretched out his hand and began his defense. **2*** "I count myself fortunate, King Agrippa, that I am to defend myself before you today against all the charges made against me by the Jews, **3** especially since you are an expert in all the Jewish customs and controversies. And therefore I beg you to listen patiently. **4** My manner of living from my youth, a life spent from the beginning among my people* and in Jerusalem, all [the] Jews know. **5a** They have known about me from the start, if they are willing to testify, that I have lived my life as a Pharisee, the strictest party of our religion. **6b** But now I am standing trial because of my hope in the promise made by God to our ancestors. **7** Our twelve tribes hope to attain to that promise as they fervently worship God day and night; and on account of this hope I am accused by Jews, O king. **8** Why is it thought unbelievable among you that God raises the dead? **9c** I myself once thought that I had to do many things against the name of Jesus the Nazorean, **10d** and I did so in Jerusalem. I imprisoned many of the holy ones with the authorization I received from the chief priests, and when they were to be put to death I cast my vote against them. **11** Many times, in synagogue after synagogue, I punished them in an attempt to force them to blaspheme; I was so enraged against them that I pursued them even to foreign cities.

a. [26:5] Phil 3:5–6; Gal 1:13–14;
   2Cor 11:22.
b. [26:6–8] 23:6; 24:15, 21; 28:20.
c. [26:9–11] 8:3; 9:1–2; 22:19; Phil 3:6.
d. [26:10] 9:14.

Read Acts 26:24–32

Paul's speech elicits various reactions. King Agrippa notes that Paul could have been freed had he not appealed to Caesar.

Reflect: Notice the reactions and dialogue in this section.

Pray: Paul believes that King Agrippa will be converted. Pray for others to convert to the Christian faith.

Act: King Agrippa appears exasperated by this experience, yet his exasperation does not blind him to the fact that Paul is innocent of wrongdoing. When I find myself in situations that exasperate me, does that exasperation blind my judgment?

12 "On one such occasion I was traveling to Damascus with the authorization and commission of the chief priests. 13e At midday, along the way, O king, I saw a light from the sky, brighter than the sun, shining around me and my traveling companions.f 14g We all fell to the ground and I heard a voice saying to me in Hebrew, 'Saul, Saul, why are you persecuting me? It is hard for you to kick against the goad.'* 15h And I said, 'Who are you, sir?' And the Lord replied, 'I am Jesus whom you are persecuting. 16i Get up now, and stand on your feet. I have appeared to you for this purpose, to appoint you as a servant and witness of what you have seen [of me] and what you will be shown.* 17j I shall deliver you from this people and from the Gentiles to whom I send you, 18k to open their eyes* that they may turn from darkness to light and from the power of Satan to God, so that they may obtain forgiveness of sins and an inheritance among those who have been consecrated by faith in me.'

19 "And so, King Agrippa, I was not disobedient to the heavenly vision. 20 On the contrary, first to those in Damascus and in Jerusalem and throughout the whole country of Judea, and then to the Gentiles, I preached the need to repent and turn to God, and to do works giving evidence of repentance. 21l That is why the Jews seized me [when I was] in the temple and tried to kill me. 22m But I have enjoyed God's help to this very day, and so I stand here testifying to small and great alike, saying nothing different from what the prophets and Moses foretold,* 23n that the Messiah must suffer* and that, as the first to rise from the dead, he would proclaim light both to our people and to the Gentiles."

Reactions to Paul's Speech.

24 While Paul was so speaking in his defense, Festus said in a loud voice, "You are mad, Paul; much learning is driving you mad." 25 But Paul replied, "I am not mad, most excellent Festus; I am speaking words of truth and reason. 26 The king knows about these matters and to him I speak boldly, for I cannot believe that [any] of this has escaped his notice; this was not done in a corner.* 27 King Agrippa, do you believe the prophets?* I know you believe." 28 Then Agrippa said to Paul, "You will soon persuade me to play the Christian." 29 Paul replied, "I would pray to God that sooner or later not only you but all who listen to me today might become as I am except for these chains."

30 Then the king rose, and with him the governor and Bernice and the others who sat with them. 31* And after they had withdrawn they said to one another, "This man is doing nothing [at all] that deserves death or impris-

e. [26:13–14] 9:7.
f. [26:13] 9:3; 22:6.
g. [26:14] 9:4; 22:7.
h. [26:15] 9:5; 22:8; Mt 25:40.
i. [26:16] 9:6; 22:10; Ez 2:1.
j. [26:17] Jer 1:7.
k. [26:18] Is 42:7, 16; 61:1 LXX; Col 1:13.
l. [26:21] 21:31.
m. [26:22–23] 3:18; Lk 24:26–27, 44–47.
n. [26:23] Is 42:6; 49:6; Lk 2:32;
    1Cor 15:20–23.

onment." **32o** And Agrippa said to Festus, "This man could have been set free if he had not appealed to Caesar."

Departure for Rome.

27 **1*** When it was decided that we should sail to Italy, they handed Paul and some other prisoners over to a centurion named Julius of the Cohort Augusta.* **2a** We went on board a ship from Adramyttium bound for ports in the province of Asia and set sail. Aristarchus, a Macedonian from Thessalonica, was with us. **3** On the following day we put in at Sidon where Julius was kind enough to allow Paul to visit his friends who took care of him. **4** From there we put out to sea and sailed around the sheltered side of Cyprus because of the headwinds, **5** and crossing the open sea off the coast of Cilicia and Pamphylia we came to Myra in Lycia.

Storm and Shipwreck.

6 There the centurion found an Alexandrian ship that was sailing to Italy and put us on board. **7** For many days we made little headway, arriving at Cnidus only with difficulty, and because the wind would not permit us to continue our course we sailed for the sheltered side of Crete off Salmone. **8** We sailed past it with difficulty and reached a place called Fair Havens, near which was the city of Lasea.

9b Much time had now passed and sailing had become hazardous because the time of the fast* had already gone by, so Paul warned them, **10** "Men, I can see that this voyage will result in severe damage and heavy loss not only to the cargo and the ship, but also to our lives." **11** The centurion, however, paid more attention to the pilot and to the owner of the ship than to what Paul said. **12** Since the harbor was unfavorably situated for spending the winter, the majority planned to put out to sea from there in the hope of reaching Phoenix, a port in Crete facing west-northwest, there to spend the winter. **13** A south wind blew gently, and thinking they had attained their objective, they weighed anchor and sailed along close to the coast of Crete. **14** Before long an offshore wind of hurricane force called a "Northeaster" struck. **15** Since the ship was caught up in it and could not head into the wind we gave way and let ourselves be driven. **16** We passed along the sheltered side of an island named Cauda and managed only with difficulty to get the dinghy under control. **17** They hoisted it aboard, then used cables to undergird the ship. Because of their fear that they would run aground on the shoal of Syrtis, they lowered the drift anchor and were carried along in this way. **18** We were being pounded by

---

Read Acts 27:1–28

A sailing adventure is described in great detail. Even though Paul is held captive on the ship, he is able to get along well with his captors and save the lives of those on board during the storm.

Reflect: Compare this sailing story with that in the first chapter of the book of Jonah. While Jonah's presence creates a problem, Paul's presence has the opposite effect.

Pray: The image of a ship weathering a tempest or storm is often used to symbolically illustrate the experience of faith. Pray for the calm and reassuring spirit that Paul exhibited on this difficult journey.

Act: Paul was not bitter about his experience or the reason why he was on this ship. Put aside bitter feelings that you may have and be willing to embrace new challenges while "sailing on the seas of faith."

---

o. [26:32] 25:11–12.

a. [27:2] 19:29; 20:4.
b. [27:9] Lv 16:29–31.

Read Acts 27:29–44

The shipwreck is described. The soldiers spare the lives of the prisoners and all 276 people on board survive.

Reflect: Even though Paul is not celebrating the Eucharist, his actions as described in verses 35–36 have eucharistic overtones.

Pray: In the midst of adversity and hardship, Paul remained positive, upbeat, and optimistic. Pray for that same type of outlook in your own life.

Act: Remember to give thanks to God each time you eat, even if all you can offer is a short and simple prayer.

the storm so violently that the next day they jettisoned some cargo, ¹⁹ and on the third day with their own hands they threw even the ship's tackle overboard. ²⁰ Neither the sun nor the stars were visible for many days, and no small storm raged. Finally, all hope of our surviving was taken away.

²¹ When many would no longer eat, Paul stood among them and said, "Men, you should have taken my advice and not have set sail from Crete and you would have avoided this disastrous loss. ²² I urge you now to keep up your courage; not one of you will be lost, only the ship. ²³ For last night an angel of the God to whom [I] belong and whom I serve stood by me ^{24c} and said, 'Do not be afraid, Paul. You are destined to stand before Caesar; and behold, for your sake, God has granted safety to all who are sailing with you.' ²⁵ Therefore, keep up your courage, men; I trust in God that it will turn out as I have been told. ²⁶ We are destined to run aground on some island."

²⁷ On the fourteenth night, as we were still being driven about on the Adriatic Sea, toward midnight the sailors began to suspect that they were nearing land. ²⁸ They took soundings and found twenty fathoms; a little farther on, they again took soundings and found fifteen fathoms. ²⁹ Fearing that we would run aground on a rocky coast, they dropped four anchors from the stern and prayed for day to come. ³⁰ The sailors then tried to abandon ship; they lowered the dinghy to the sea on the pretext of going to lay out anchors from the bow. ³¹ But Paul said to the centurion and the soldiers, "Unless these men stay with the ship, you cannot be saved." ³² So the soldiers cut the ropes of the dinghy and set it adrift.

³³ Until the day began to dawn, Paul kept urging all to take some food. He said, "Today is the fourteenth day that you have been waiting, going hungry and eating nothing. ³⁴ I urge you, therefore, to take some food; it will help you survive. Not a hair of the head of anyone of you will be lost." ^{35d} When he said this, he took bread,* gave thanks to God in front of them all, broke it, and began to eat. ³⁶ They were all encouraged, and took some food themselves. ³⁷ In all, there were two hundred seventy-six of us on the ship. ³⁸ After they had eaten enough, they lightened the ship by throwing the wheat into the sea.

³⁹ When day came they did not recognize the land, but made out a bay with a beach. They planned to run the ship ashore on it, if they could. ⁴⁰ So they cast off the anchors and abandoned them to the sea, and at the same time they unfastened the lines of the rudders, and hoisting the foresail into the wind, they made for the

c. [27:24] 23:11.
d. [27:35] Mt 15:36; Mk 6:41; 8:6; Lk 22:19; 1Cor 11:23–24.

beach. [41] But they struck a sandbar and ran the ship aground. The bow was wedged in and could not be moved, but the stern began to break up under the pounding [of the waves]. [42] The soldiers planned to kill the prisoners so that none might swim away and escape, [43] but the centurion wanted to save Paul and so kept them from carrying out their plan. He ordered those who could swim to jump overboard first and get to the shore, [44] and then the rest, some on planks, others on debris from the ship. In this way, all reached shore safely.

Winter in Malta.

28 [1] Once we had reached safety we learned that the island was called Malta. [2] The natives showed us extraordinary hospitality; they lit a fire and welcomed all of us because it had begun to rain and was cold. [3] Paul had gathered a bundle of brushwood and was putting it on the fire when a viper, escaping from the heat, fastened on his hand. [4] When the natives saw the snake hanging from his hand, they said to one another, "This man must certainly be a murderer; though he escaped the sea, Justice* has not let him remain alive." [5] But he shook the snake off into the fire and suffered no harm. [6a] They were expecting him to swell up or suddenly to fall down dead but, after waiting a long time and seeing nothing unusual happen to him, they changed their minds and began to say that he was a god. [7] In the vicinity of that place were lands belonging to a man named Publius, the chief of the island. He welcomed us and received us cordially as his guests for three days. [8] It so happened that the father of Publius was sick with a fever and dysentery. Paul visited him and, after praying, laid his hands on him and healed him. [9] After this had taken place, the rest of the sick on the island came to Paul and were cured. [10] They paid us great honor and when we eventually set sail they brought us the provisions we needed.

Arrival in Rome.

[11] Three months later we set sail on a ship that had wintered at the island. It was an Alexandrian ship with the Dioscuri* as its figurehead. [12] We put in at Syracuse and stayed there three days, [13] and from there we sailed round the coast and arrived at Rhegium. After a day, a south wind came up and in two days we reached Puteoli. [14] There we found some brothers and were urged to stay with them for seven days. And thus we came to Rome. [15] The brothers from there heard about us and came as far as the Forum of Appius and Three Taverns to meet us. On seeing them, Paul gave thanks to God

a. [28:6] 14:11.

Read Acts 28:17–31

Paul testifies among the Jews of Rome and insists that he did not act contrary to Jewish laws, tradition, or customs. For a third time (see Acts 13:44–52 and Acts 18:5–6), the theme of the Jews rejecting the good news preached by Paul and the subsequent direction of his efforts to the Gentiles is presented.

Reflect: Paul's quote of Isaiah 6:9–10 attempts to explain how the salvation promised in the Old Testament and brought forth in the person of Jesus was offered to the Jewish people but has been accepted by the Gentiles. What is our spiritual kinship with those who have not accepted Jesus as the messiah?

Pray: Mindful of our Judeo-Christian tradition, let us pray for our Jewish brothers and sisters, especially on their holy days and during their special observances (e.g., Passover, Yom Kippur, Rosh Hashanah, Chanukah).

Act: Being a witness and giving testimony are important themes that have recurred in the Acts of the Apostles. In what specific ways do you see yourself imitating the example and following in the footsteps of the two great leaders of the early church, Peter and Paul?

---

and took courage. **16** When he entered Rome,* Paul was allowed to live by himself, with the soldier who was guarding him.

Testimony to Jews in Rome.

17*b Three days later he called together the leaders of the Jews. When they had gathered he said to them, "My brothers, although I had done nothing against our people or our ancestral customs, I was handed over to the Romans as a prisoner from Jerusalem. **18c** After trying my case the Romans wanted to release me, because they found nothing against me deserving the death penalty. **19d** But when the Jews objected, I was obliged to appeal to Caesar, even though I had no accusation to make against my own nation. **20e** This is the reason, then, I have requested to see you and to speak with you, for it is on account of the hope of Israel* that I wear these chains." **21** They answered him, "We have received no letters from Judea about you, nor has any of the brothers arrived with a damaging report or rumor about you. **22f** But we should like to hear you present your views, for we know that this sect is denounced everywhere."

23 So they arranged a day with him and came to his lodgings in great numbers. From early morning until evening, he expounded his position to them, bearing witness to the kingdom of God and trying to convince them about Jesus from the law of Moses and the prophets. **24** Some were convinced by what he had said, while others did not believe. **25*** Without reaching any agreement among themselves they began to leave; then Paul made one final statement. "Well did the holy Spirit speak to your ancestors through the prophet Isaiah, saying:

26g 'Go to this people and say:
You shall indeed hear but not understand.
      You shall indeed look but never see.
27 Gross is the heart of this people;
      they will not hear with their ears;
      they have closed their eyes,
      so they may not see with their eyes
      and hear with their ears
and understand with their heart and be converted,
      and I heal them.'

28h Let it be known to you that this salvation of God has been sent to the Gentiles; they will listen." **29***

30* He remained for two full years in his lodgings. He received all who came to him, **31** and with complete assurance and without hindrance he proclaimed the kingdom of God and taught about the Lord Jesus Christ.

b. [28:17] 24:12–13; 25:8.
c. [28:18] 23:29; 25:25; 26:31–32.
d. [28:19] 25:11.
e. [28:20] 23:6; 24:15, 21; 26:6–8.
f. [28:22] 24:5, 14.
g. [28:26] Is 6:9–10; Mt 13:14–15; Mk 4:12; Lk 8:10; Jn 12:40; Rom 11:8.
h. [28:28] 13:46; 18:6; Ps 67:2; Is 40:5 LXX; Lk 3:6.

CHAPTER 1

*1[1–26] This introductory material (Acts 1:1–2) connects Acts with the Gospel of Luke, shows that the apostles were instructed by the risen Jesus (Acts 1:3–5), points out that the parousia or second coming in glory of Jesus will occur as certainly as his ascension occurred (Acts 1:6–11), and lists the members of the Twelve, stressing their role as a body of divinely mandated witnesses to his life, teaching, and resurrection (Acts 1:12–26).

*[3] **Appearing to them during forty days**: Luke considered especially sacred the interval in which the appearances and instructions of the risen Jesus occurred and expressed it therefore in terms of the sacred number forty (cf. Dt 8:2). In his gospel, however, Luke connects the ascension of Jesus with the resurrection by describing the ascension on Easter Sunday evening (Lk 24:50–53). What should probably be understood as one event (resurrection, glorification, ascension, sending of the Spirit—the paschal mystery) has been historicized by Luke when he writes of a visible ascension of Jesus after forty days and the descent of the Spirit at Pentecost. For Luke, the ascension marks the end of the appearances of Jesus except for the extraordinary appearance to Paul. With regard to Luke's understanding of salvation history, the ascension also marks the end of the time of Jesus (Lk 24:50–53) and signals the beginning of the time of the church.

*[4] **The promise of the Father**: the holy Spirit, as is clear from the next verse. This gift of the Spirit was first promised in Jesus' final instructions to his chosen witnesses in Luke's gospel (Lk 24:49) and formed part of the continuing instructions of the risen Jesus on the kingdom of God, of which Luke speaks in Acts 1:3.

*[6] The question of the disciples implies that in believing Jesus to be the Christ (see note on Lk 2:11) they had expected him to be a political leader who would restore self-rule to Israel during his historical ministry. When this had not taken place, they ask if it is to take place at this time, the period of the church.

*[7] This verse echoes the tradition that the precise time of the parousia is not revealed to human beings; cf. Mk 13:32; 1Thes 5:1–3.

*[8] Just as Jerusalem was the city of destiny in the Gospel of Luke (the place where salvation was accomplished), so here at the beginning of Acts, Jerusalem occupies a central position. It is the starting point for the mission of the Christian disciples to "the ends of the earth," the place where the apostles were situated and the doctrinal focal point in the early days of the community (Acts 15:2, 6). **The ends of the earth**: for Luke, this means Rome.

*[18] Luke records a popular tradition about the death of Judas that differs from the one in Mt 27:5, according to which Judas hanged himself. Here, although the text is not certain, Judas is depicted as purchasing a piece of property with the betrayal money and being killed on it in a fall.

*[26] The need to replace Judas was probably dictated by the symbolism of the number twelve, recalling the twelve tribes of Israel. This symbolism also indicates that for Luke (see Lk 22:30) the Christian church is a reconstituted Israel.

CHAPTER 2

*2[1–41] Luke's pentecostal narrative consists of an introduction (Acts 2:1–13), a speech ascribed to Peter declaring the resurrection of Jesus and its messianic significance (Acts 2:14–36), and a favorable response from the audience (Acts 2:37–41). It is likely that the narrative telescopes events that took place over a period of time and on a less dramatic scale. The Twelve were not originally in a position to proclaim pub-

licly the messianic office of Jesus without incurring immediate reprisal from those religious authorities in Jerusalem who had brought about Jesus' death precisely to stem the rising tide in his favor.

*[2] **There came from the sky a noise like a strong driving wind**: wind and spirit are associated in Jn 3:8. The sound of a great rush of wind would herald a new action of God in the history of salvation.

*[3] **Tongues as of fire**: see Ex 19:18 where fire symbolizes the presence of God to initiate the covenant on Sinai. Here the holy Spirit acts upon the apostles, preparing them to proclaim the new covenant with its unique gift of the Spirit (Acts 2:38).

*[4] **To speak in different tongues**: ecstatic prayer in praise of God, interpreted in Acts 2:6, 11 as speaking in foreign languages, symbolizing the worldwide mission of the church.

*[14–36] The first of six discourses in Acts (along with Acts 3:12–26; 4:8–12; 5:29–32; 10:34–43; 13:16–41) dealing with the resurrection of Jesus and its messianic import. Five of these are attributed to Peter, the final one to Paul. Modern scholars term these discourses in Acts the "kerygma," the Greek word for proclamation (cf. 1Cor 15:11).

*[33] **At the right hand of God**: or "by the right hand of God."

*[38] **Repent and be baptized**: repentance is a positive concept, a change of mind and heart toward God reflected in the actual goodness of one's life. It is in accord with the apostolic teaching derived from Jesus (Acts 2:42) and ultimately recorded in the four gospels. Luke presents baptism in Acts as the expected response to the apostolic preaching about Jesus and associates it with the conferring of the Spirit (Acts 1:5; 10:44–48; 11:16).

*[42–47] The first of three summary passages (along with Acts 4:32–37; 5:12–16) that outline, somewhat idyllically, the chief characteristics of the Jerusalem community: adherence to the teachings of the Twelve and the centering of its religious life in the eucharistic liturgy (Acts 2:42); a system of distribution of goods that led wealthier Christians to sell their possessions when the needs of the community's poor required it (Acts 2:44 and the note on Acts 4:32–37); and continued attendance at the temple, since in this initial stage there was little or no thought of any dividing line between Christianity and Judaism (Acts 2:46).

CHAPTER 3

*3[1]–4[31] This section presents a series of related events: the dramatic cure of a lame beggar (Acts 3:1–10) produces a large audience for the kerygmatic discourse of Peter (Acts 3:11–26). The Sadducees, taking exception to the doctrine of resurrection, have Peter, John, and apparently the beggar as well, arrested (Acts 4:1–4) and brought to trial before the Sanhedrin. The issue concerns the authority by which Peter and John publicly teach religious doctrine in the temple (Acts 4:5–7). Peter replies with a brief summary of the kerygma, implying that his authority is prophetic (Acts 4:8–12). The court warns the apostles to abandon their practice of invoking prophetic authority in the name of Jesus (Acts 4:13–18). When Peter and John reply that the prophetic role cannot be abandoned to satisfy human objections, the court nevertheless releases them, afraid to do otherwise since the beggar, lame from birth and over forty years old, is a well-known figure in Jerusalem and the facts of his cure are common property (Acts 4:19–22). The narrative concludes with a prayer of the Christian community imploring divine aid against threats of persecution (Acts 4:23–31).

*3[1] **For the three o'clock hour of prayer**: literally, "at the ninth hour of prayer." With the day beginning at 6 A.M., the ninth hour would be 3 P.M.

*[6–10] The miracle has a dramatic cast; it symbolizes the saving

power of Christ and leads the beggar to enter the temple, where he hears Peter's proclamation of salvation through Jesus.

*[13] **Has glorified**: through the resurrection and ascension of Jesus, God reversed the judgment against him on the occasion of his trial. **Servant**: the Greek word can also be rendered as "son" or even "child" here and also in Acts 3:26; 4:25 (applied to David); Acts 4:27; and Acts 4:30. Scholars are of the opinion, however, that the original concept reflected in the words identified Jesus with the suffering Servant of the Lord of Is 52:13–53:12.

*[14] **The Holy and Righteous One**: so designating Jesus emphasizes his special relationship to the Father (see Lk 1:35; 4:34) and emphasizes his sinlessness and religious dignity that are placed in sharp contrast with the guilt of those who rejected him in favor of Barabbas.

*[15] **The author of life**: other possible translations of the Greek title are "leader of life" or "pioneer of life." The title clearly points to Jesus as the source and originator of salvation.

*[17] **Ignorance**: a Lucan motif, explaining away the actions not only of the people but also of their leaders in crucifying Jesus. On this basis the presbyters in Acts could continue to appeal to the Jews in Jerusalem to believe in Jesus, even while affirming their involvement in his death because they were unaware of his messianic dignity. See also Acts 13:27 and Lk 23:34.

*[18] **Through the mouth of all the prophets**: Christian prophetic insight into the Old Testament saw the crucifixion and death of Jesus as the main import of messianic prophecy. The Jews themselves did not anticipate a suffering Messiah; they usually understood the Servant Song in Is 52:13—53:12 to signify their own suffering as a people. In his typical fashion (cf. Lk 18:31; 24:25, 27, 44), Luke does not specify the particular Old Testament prophecies that were fulfilled by Jesus. See also note on Lk 24:26.

*[20] **The Lord ... and send you the Messiah already appointed for you, Jesus**: an allusion to the parousia or second coming of Christ, judged to be imminent in the apostolic age. This reference to its nearness is the only explicit one in Acts. Some scholars believe that this verse preserves a very early christology, in which the title "Messiah" (Greek "Christ") is applied to him as of his parousia, his second coming (contrast Acts 2:36). This view of a future messiahship of Jesus is not found elsewhere in the New Testament.

*[21] **The times of universal restoration**: like "the times of refreshment" (Acts 3:20), an apocalyptic designation of the messianic age, fitting in with the christology of Acts 3:20 that associates the messiahship of Jesus with his future coming.

*[22] A loose citation of Dt 18:15, which teaches that the Israelites are to learn the will of Yahweh from no one but their prophets. At the time of Jesus, some Jews expected a unique prophet to come in fulfillment of this text. Early Christianity applied this tradition and text to Jesus and used them especially in defense of the divergence of Christian teaching from traditional Judaism.

CHAPTER 4

*4[1] **The priests, the captain of the temple guard, and the Sadducees**: the priests performed the temple liturgy; the temple guard was composed of Levites, whose captain ranked next after the high priest. The Sadducees, a party within Judaism at this time, rejected those doctrines, including bodily resurrection, which they believed alien to the ancient Mosaic religion. The Sadducees were drawn from priestly families and from the lay aristocracy.

*[11] Early Christianity applied this citation from Ps 118:22 to Jesus; cf. Mk 12:10; 1Pt 2:7.

*[12] In the Roman world of Luke's day, salvation was often attributed to the emperor who was hailed as "savior" and "god." Luke, in the words of Peter, denies that deliverance comes through anyone other than Jesus.

*[27] **Herod**: Herod Antipas, ruler of Galilee and Perea from 4 B.C. to A.D. 39, who executed John the Baptist and before whom Jesus was arraigned; cf. Lk 23:6–12.

*[31] **The place... shook**: the earthquake is used as a sign of the divine presence in Ex 19:18; Is 6:4. Here the shaking of the building symbolizes God's favorable response to the prayer. Luke may have had as an additional reason for using the symbol in this sense the fact that it was familiar in the Hellenistic world. Ovid and Virgil also employ it.

*[32–37] This is the second summary characterizing the Jerusalem community (see note on Acts 2:42–47). It emphasizes the system of the distribution of goods and introduces Barnabas, who appears later in Acts as the friend and companion of Paul, and who, as noted here (Acts 4:37), endeared himself to the community by a donation of money through the sale of property. This sharing of material possessions continues a practice that Luke describes during the historical ministry of Jesus (Lk 8:3) and is in accord with the sayings of Jesus in Luke's gospel (Lk 12:33; 16:9, 11, 13).

CHAPTER 5

* 5[1–11] The sin of Ananias and Sapphira did not consist in the withholding of part of the money but in their deception of the community. Their deaths are ascribed to a lie to the holy Spirit (Acts 5:3, 9), i.e., they accepted the honor accorded them by the community for their generosity, but in reality they were not deserving of it.

* [12–16] This, the third summary portraying the Jerusalem community, underscores the Twelve as its bulwark, especially because of their charismatic power to heal the sick; cf. Acts 2:42–47; 4:32–37.

* [17–42] A second action against the community is taken by the Sanhedrin in the arrest and trial of the Twelve; cf. Acts 4:1–3. The motive is the jealousy of the religious authorities over the popularity of the apostles (Acts 5:17) who are now charged with the defiance of the Sanhedrin's previous order to them to abandon their prophetic role (Acts 5:28; cf. Acts 4:18). In this crisis the apostles are favored by a miraculous release from prison (Acts 5:18–24). (For similar incidents involving Peter and Paul, see Acts 12:6–11; 16:25–29.) The real significance of such an event, however, would be manifest only to people of faith, not to unbelievers; since the Sanhedrin already judged the Twelve to be inauthentic prophets, it could disregard reports of their miracles. When the Twelve immediately resumed public teaching, the Sanhedrin determined to invoke upon them the penalty of death (Acts 5:33) prescribed in Dt 13:6–10. Gamaliel's advice against this course finally prevailed, but it did not save the Twelve from the punishment of scourging (Acts 5:40) in a last endeavor to shake their conviction of their prophetic mission.

* [30] **Hanging him on a tree**: that is, crucifying him (cf. also Gal 3:13).

* [31] **At his right hand**: see note on Acts 2:33.

* [34] **Gamaliel**: in Acts 22:3, Paul identifies himself as a disciple of this Rabbi Gamaliel I who flourished in Jerusalem between A.D. 25 and 50.

* [36–37] Gamaliel offers examples of unsuccessful contemporary movements to argue that if God is not the origin of this movement preached by the apostles it will perish by itself. The movement initiated by Theudas actually occurred when C. Cuspius Fadus was governor, A.D. 44–46. Luke's placing of Judas the Galilean after Theudas and at the time of the census (see note on Lk 2:1–2) is an indication of the vagueness of his knowledge of these events.

CHAPTER 6

* 6[1–7] **The Hellenists ... the Hebrews**: the Hellenists were not necessarily Jews from the diaspora, but were more probably Palestinian Jews who spoke only Greek. The Hebrews were Palestinian Jews who spoke Hebrew or Aramaic and who may also have spoken Greek. Both groups

belong to the Jerusalem Jewish Christian community. The conflict between them leads to a restructuring of the community that will better serve the community's needs. The real purpose of the whole episode, however, is to introduce Stephen as a prominent figure in the community whose long speech and martyrdom will be recounted in Acts 7.

* [2–4] The essential function of the Twelve is the "service of the word," including development of the kerygma by formulation of the teachings of Jesus.

* [2] To serve at table: some commentators think that it is not the serving of food that is described here but rather the keeping of the accounts that recorded the distribution of food to the needy members of the community. In any case, after Stephen and the others are chosen, they are never presented carrying out the task for which they were appointed (Acts 6:2–3). Rather, two of their number, Stephen and Philip, are presented as preachers of the Christian message. They, the Hellenist counterpart of the Twelve, are active in the ministry of the word.

* [6] They ... laid hands on them: the customary Jewish way of designating persons for a task and invoking upon them the divine blessing and power to perform it.

* 6[8]—8[1] The summary (Acts 6:7) on the progress of the Jerusalem community, illustrated by the conversion of the priests, is followed by a lengthy narrative regarding Stephen. Stephen's defense is not a response to the charges made against him but takes the form of a discourse that reviews the fortunes of God's word to Israel and leads to a prophetic declaration: a plea for the hearing of that word as announced by Christ and now possessed by the Christian community.

The charges that Stephen depreciated the importance of the temple and the Mosaic law and elevated Jesus to a stature above Moses (Acts 6:13–14) were in fact true. Before the Sanhedrin, no defense against them was possible. With Stephen, who thus perceived the fuller implications of the teachings of Jesus, the differences between Judaism and Christianity began to appear. Luke's account of Stephen's martyrdom and its aftermath shows how the major impetus behind the Christian movement passed from Jerusalem, where the temple and law prevailed, to Antioch in Syria, where these influences were less pressing.

* [13] False witnesses: here, and in his account of Stephen's execution (Acts 7:54–60), Luke parallels the martyrdom of Stephen with the death of Jesus.

CHAPTER 7

* 7[2–53] Stephen's speech represents Luke's description of Christianity's break from its Jewish matrix. Two motifs become prominent in the speech: (Acts 7:1) Israel's reaction to God's chosen leaders in the past reveals that the people have consistently rejected them; and (Acts 7:2) Israel has misunderstood God's choice of the Jerusalem temple as the place where he is to be worshiped.

* [2] God ... appeared to our father Abraham ... in Mesopotamia: the first of a number of minor discrepancies between the data of the Old Testament and the data of Stephen's discourse. According to Gn 12:1, God first spoke to Abraham in Haran. The main discrepancies are these: in Acts 7:16 it is said that Jacob was buried in Shechem, whereas Gn 50:13 says he was buried at Hebron; in the same verse it is said that the tomb was purchased by Abraham, but in Gn 33:19 and Jos 24:32 the purchase is attributed to Jacob himself.

* [55] He ... saw ... Jesus standing at the right hand of God: Stephen affirms to the Sanhedrin that the prophecy Jesus made before them has been fulfilled (Mk 14:62).

* [57] Covered their ears: Stephen's declaration, like that of Jesus, is a scandal to the court, which regards it as blasphemy.

* [59] Compare Lk 23:34, 46.

CHAPTER 8

* 8[1–40] Some idea of the severity of the persecution that now breaks out against the Jerusalem community can be gathered from Acts 22:4 and Acts 26:9–11. Luke, however, concentrates on the fortunes of the word of God among people, indicating how the dispersal of the Jewish community resulted in the conversion of the Samaritans (Acts 8:4–17, 25). His narrative is further expanded to include the account of Philip's acceptance of an Ethiopian (Acts 8:26–39).

* [1] All were scattered ... except the apostles: this observation leads some modern scholars to conclude that the persecution was limited to the Hellenist Christians and that the Hebrew Christians were not molested, perhaps because their attitude toward the law and temple was still more in line with that of their fellow Jews (see the charge leveled against the Hellenist Stephen in Acts 6:13–14). Whatever the facts, it appears that the Twelve took no public stand regarding Stephen's position, choosing, instead, to await the development of events.

* [3] Saul ... was trying to destroy the church: like Stephen, Saul was able to perceive that the Christian movement contained the seeds of doctrinal divergence from Judaism. A pupil of Gamaliel, according to Acts 22:3, and totally dedicated to the law as the way of salvation (Gal 1:13–14), Saul accepted the task of crushing the Christian movement, at least insofar as it detracted from the importance of the temple and the law. His vehement opposition to Christianity reveals how difficult it was for a Jew of his time to accept a messianism that differed so greatly from the general expectation.

* [9–13, 18–24] Sorcerers were well known in the ancient world. Probably the incident involving Simon and his altercation with Peter is introduced to show that the miraculous charisms possessed by members of the Christian community (Acts 8:6–7) were not to be confused with the magic of sorcerers.

* [16] Here and in Acts 10:44–48 and Acts 19:1–6, Luke distinguishes between baptism in the name of the Lord Jesus and the reception of the Spirit. In each case, the Spirit is conferred through members of the Twelve (Peter and John) or their representative (Paul). This may be Luke's way of describing the role of the church in the bestowal of the Spirit. Elsewhere in Acts, baptism and the Spirit are more closely related (Acts 1:5; 11:16).

* [18–20] Simon attempts to buy the gift of God (Acts 8:20) with money. Peter's cursing of Simon's attempt so to use his money expresses a typically Lucan attitude toward material wealth (cf. Lk 6:24; 12:16–21; 16:13).

* [26–40] In the account of the conversion of the Ethiopian eunuch, Luke adduces additional evidence to show that the spread of Christianity outside the confines of Judaism itself was in accord with the plan of God. He does not make clear whether the Ethiopian was originally a convert to Judaism or, as is more probable, a "God-fearer" (Acts 10:1), i.e., one who accepted Jewish monotheism and ethic and attended the synagogue but did not consider himself bound by other regulations such as circumcision and observance of the dietary laws. The story of his conversion to Christianity is given a strong supernatural cast by the introduction of an angel (Acts 8:26), instruction from the holy Spirit (Acts 8:29), and the strange removal of Philip from the scene (8:39).

* [27] The Candace: Candace is not a proper name here but the title of a Nubian queen.

* [30–34] Philip is brought alongside the carriage at the very moment when the Ethiopian is pondering the meaning of Is 53:7–8, a passage that Christianity, from its earliest origins, has applied to Jesus; cf. note on Acts 3:13.

* [37] The oldest and best manuscripts of Acts omit this verse, which is a Western text reading: "And Philip said, 'If you believe with all your heart, you may.' And he said in reply, 'I believe that Jesus Christ is the Son of God.'"

CHAPTER 9

* **9[1–19]** This is the first of three accounts of Paul's conversion (with Acts 22:3–16 and Acts 26:2–18) with some differences of detail owing to Luke's use of different sources. Paul's experience was not visionary but was precipitated by the appearance of Jesus, as he insists in 1Cor 15:8. The words of Jesus, "Saul, Saul, why are you persecuting me?" related by Luke with no variation in all three accounts, exerted a profound and lasting influence on the thought of Paul. Under the influence of this experience he gradually developed his understanding of justification by faith (see the letters to the Galatians and Romans) and of the identification of the Christian community with Jesus Christ (see 1Cor 12:27). That Luke would narrate this conversion three times is testimony to the importance he attaches to it. This first account occurs when the word is first spread to the Gentiles. At this point, the conversion of the hero of the Gentile mission is recounted. The emphasis in the account is on Paul as a divinely chosen instrument (Acts 9:15).

* **[2] The Way**: a name used by the early Christian community for itself (Acts 18:26; 19:9, 23; 22:4; 24:14, 22). The Essene community at Qumran used the same designation to describe its mode of life.

* **[8] He could see nothing**: a temporary blindness (Acts 9:18) symbolizing the religious blindness of Saul as persecutor (cf. Acts 26:18).

* **[13] Your holy ones**: literally, "your saints."

* **[19–30]** This is a brief resume of Paul's initial experience as an apostolic preacher. At first he found himself in the position of being regarded as an apostate by the Jews and suspect by the Christian community of Jerusalem. His acceptance by the latter was finally brought about through his friendship with Barnabas (Acts 9:27).

* **[20] Son of God**: the title "Son of God" occurs in Acts only here, but cf. the citation of Ps 2:7 in Paul's speech at Antioch in Pisidia (Acts 13:33).

* **[26]** This visit of Paul to Jerusalem is mentioned by Paul in Gal 1:18.

* **[29] Hellenists**: see note on Acts 6:1–7.

* **[31–43]** In the context of the period of peace enjoyed by the community through the cessation of Paul's activities against it, Luke introduces two traditions concerning the miraculous power exercised by Peter as he was making a tour of places where the Christian message had already been preached. The towns of Lydda, Sharon, and Joppa were populated by both Jews and Gentiles and their Christian communities may well have been mixed.

* **[36] Tabitha (Dorcas)**, respectively the Aramaic and Greek words for "gazelle," exemplifies the right attitude toward material possessions expressed by Jesus in the Lucan Gospel (Lk 6:30; 11:41; 12:33; 18:22; 19:8).

* **[43]** The fact that Peter lodged with a tanner would have been significant to both the Gentile and Jewish Christians, for Judaism considered the tanning occupation unclean.

CHAPTER 10

* **10[1–48]** The narrative centers on the conversion of Cornelius, a Gentile and a "God-fearer" (see note on Acts 8:26–40). Luke considers the event of great importance, as is evident from his long treatment of it. The incident is again related in Acts 11:1–18 where Peter is forced to justify his actions before the Jerusalem community and alluded to in Acts 15:7–11 where at the Jerusalem "Council" Peter supports Paul's missionary activity among the Gentiles. The narrative divides itself into a series of distinct episodes, concluding with Peter's presentation of the Christian kerygma (Acts 10:4–43) and a pentecostal experience undergone by Cornelius' household preceding their reception of baptism (Acts 10:44–48).

* **[1] The Cohort called the Italica**: this battalion was an auxil-

iary unit of archers formed originally in Italy but transferred to Syria shortly before A.D. 69.

* **[2] Used to give alms generously**: like Tabitha (Acts 9:36), Cornelius exemplifies the proper attitude toward wealth (see note on Acts 9:36).

* **[3] About three o'clock**: literally, "about the ninth hour." See note on Acts 3:1.

* **[7] A devout soldier**: by using this adjective, Luke probably intends to classify him as a "God-fearer" (see note on Acts 8:26–40).

* **[9–16]** The vision is intended to prepare Peter to share the food of Cornelius' household without qualms of conscience (Acts 10:48). The necessity of such instructions to Peter reveals that at first not even the apostles fully grasped the implications of Jesus' teaching on the law. In Acts, the initial insight belongs to Stephen.

* **[9] At about noontime**: literally, "about the sixth hour."

* **[17–23]** The arrival of the Gentile emissaries with their account of the angelic apparition illuminates Peter's vision: he is to be prepared to admit Gentiles, who were considered unclean like the animals of his vision, into the Christian community.

* **[24–27]** So impressed is Cornelius with the apparition that he invites close personal friends to join him in his meeting with Peter. But his understanding of the person he is about to meet is not devoid of superstition, suggested by his falling down before him. For a similar experience of Paul and Barnabas, see Acts 14:11–18.

* **[28]** Peter now fully understands the meaning of his vision; see note on Acts 10:17–23.

* **[30] Four days ago**: literally, "from the fourth day up to this hour."

* **[34–43]** Peter's speech to the household of Cornelius typifies early Christian preaching to Gentiles.

* **[34–35]** The revelation of God's choice of Israel to be the people of God did not mean he withheld the divine favor from other people.

* **[36–43]** These words are more directed to Luke's Christian readers than to the household of Cornelius, as indicated by the opening words, "You know." They trace the continuity between the preaching and teaching of Jesus of Nazareth and the proclamation of Jesus by the early community. The emphasis on this divinely ordained continuity (Acts 10:41) is meant to assure Luke's readers of the fidelity of Christian tradition to the words and deeds of Jesus.

* **[36] To the Israelites**: Luke, in the words of Peter, speaks of the prominent position occupied by Israel in the history of salvation.

* **[38] Jesus of Nazareth**: God's revelation of his plan for the destiny of humanity through Israel culminated in Jesus of Nazareth. Consequently, the ministry of Jesus is an integral part of God's revelation. This viewpoint explains why the early Christian communities were interested in conserving the historical substance of the ministry of Jesus, a tradition leading to the production of the four gospels.

* **[39] We are witnesses**: the apostolic testimony was not restricted to the resurrection of Jesus but also included his historical ministry. This witness, however, was theological in character; the Twelve, divinely mandated as prophets, were empowered to interpret his sayings and deeds in the light of his redemptive death and resurrection. The meaning of these words and deeds was to be made clear to the developing Christian community as the bearer of the word of salvation (cf. Acts 1:21–26). **Hanging him on a tree**: see note on 5:30.

* **[42] As judge of the living and the dead**: the apostolic preaching to the Jews appealed to their messianic hope, while the preaching to Gentiles stressed the coming divine judgment; cf. 1Thes 1:10.

* **[44]** Just as the Jewish Christians received the gift of the Spirit, so too do the Gentiles.

CHAPTER 11

* **11[1–18]** The Jewish Christians of Jerusalem were scandalized to learn of Peter's sojourn in the house of the Gentile Cornelius. Nonetheless, they had to accept the divine directions given to both Peter and Cornelius. They concluded that the setting aside of the legal barriers between Jew and Gentile was an exceptional ordinance of God to indicate that the apostolic kerygma was also to be directed to the Gentiles. Only in Acts 15 at the "Council" in Jerusalem does the evangelization of the Gentiles become the official position of the church leadership in Jerusalem.
* **[3] You entered . . .:** alternatively, this could be punctuated as a question.
* **[12] These six brothers:** companions from the Christian community of Joppa (see Acts 10:23).
* **[19–26]** The Jewish Christian antipathy to the mixed community was reflected by the early missionaries generally. The few among them who entertained a different view succeeded in introducing Gentiles into the community at Antioch (in Syria). When the disconcerted Jerusalem community sent Barnabas to investigate, he was so favorably impressed by what he observed that he persuaded his friend Saul to participate in the Antioch mission.
* **[26] Christians:** "Christians" is first applied to the members of the community at Antioch because the Gentile members of the community enable it to stand out clearly from Judaism.
* **[27–30]** It is not clear whether the prophets from Jerusalem came to Antioch to request help in view of the coming famine or whether they received this insight during their visit there. The former supposition seems more likely. Suetonius and Tacitus speak of famines during the reign of Claudius (A.D. 41–54), while the Jewish historian Josephus mentions a famine in Judea in A.D. 46–48. Luke is interested, rather, in showing the charity of the Antiochene community toward the Jewish Christians of Jerusalem despite their differences on mixed communities.
* **[30] Presbyters:** this is the same Greek word that elsewhere is translated "elders," primarily in reference to the Jewish community.

CHAPTER 12

* **12[1–19]** Herod Agrippa ruled Judea A.D. 41–44. While Luke does not assign a motive for his execution of James and his intended execution of Peter, the broad background lies in Herod's support of Pharisaic Judaism. The Jewish Christians had lost the popularity they had had in Jerusalem (Acts 2:47), perhaps because of suspicions against them traceable to the teaching of Stephen.
* **[2] James, the brother of John:** this James, the son of Zebedee, was beheaded by Herod Agrippa ca. A.D. 44.
* **[3, 4] Feast of Unleavened Bread ... Passover:** see note on Lk 22:1.
* **[17] To James:** this James is not the son of Zebedee mentioned in Acts 12:2, but is James, the "brother of the Lord" (Gal 1:19), who in Acts 15; 21 is presented as leader of the Jerusalem Christian community. **He left and went to another place:** the conjecture that Peter left for Rome at this time has nothing to recommend it. His chief responsibility was still the leadership of the Jewish Christian community in Palestine (see Gal 2:7). The concept of the great missionary effort of the church was yet to come (see Acts 13:1–3).
* **[20–23]** Josephus gives a similar account of Herod's death that occurred in A.D. 44. Early Christian tradition considered the manner of it to be a divine punishment upon his evil life. See 2Kgs 19:35 for the figure of the angel of the Lord in such a context.
* **[25] They returned to Jerusalem:** many manuscripts read "from Jerusalem," since Acts 11:30 implies that Paul and Barnabas are already in Jerusalem. This present verse could refer to a return visit or subsequent relief mission.

CHAPTER 13

* **13[1–3]** The impulse for the first missionary effort in Asia Minor is ascribed to the prophets of the Antiochene community, under the inspiration of the holy Spirit. Just as the Jerusalem community had earlier been the center of missionary activity, so too Antioch becomes the center from which the missionaries Barnabas and Saul are sent out.
* **13[4]—14[27]** The key event in Luke's account of the first missionary journey is the experience of Paul and Barnabas at Pisidian Antioch. The Christian kerygma proclaimed by Paul in the synagogue was favorably received. Some Jews and "God-fearers" (see note on Acts 8:26–40) became interested and invited the missionaries to speak again on the following sabbath (Acts 13:42). By that time, however, the appearance of a large number of Gentiles from the city had so disconcerted the Jews that they became hostile toward the apostles (Acts 13:44–50). This hostility of theirs appears in all three accounts of Paul's missionary journeys in Acts, the Jews of Iconium (Acts 14:1–2) and Beroea (Acts 17:11) being notable exceptions.
* **[5] John:** that is, John Mark (see Acts 12:12, 25).
* **[6] A magician named Bar-Jesus who was a Jewish false prophet:** that is, he posed as a prophet. Again Luke takes the opportunity to dissociate Christianity from the magical acts of the time (Acts 13:7–11); see also Acts 8:18–24.
* **[9] Saul, also known as Paul:** there is no reason to believe that his name was changed from Saul to Paul upon his conversion. The use of a double name, one Semitic (Saul), the other Greco-Roman (Paul), is well attested (cf. Acts 1:23, Joseph Justus; Acts 12:12, 25, John Mark).
* **[16–41]** This is the first of several speeches of Paul to Jews proclaiming that the Christian church is the logical development of Pharisaic Judaism (see also Acts 24:10–21; 26:2–23).
* **[16] Who are God-fearing:** see note on Acts 8:26–40.
* **[18] Put up with:** some manuscripts read "sustained."
* **[20] At the end of about four hundred and fifty years:** the manuscript tradition is uncertain whether the mention of four hundred and fifty years refers to the sojourn in Egypt before the Exodus, the wilderness period and the time of the conquest (see Ex 12:40–41), as the translation here suggests, or to the time between the conquest and the time of Samuel, the period of the judges, if the text is read, "After these things, for about four hundred and fifty years, he provided judges."
* **[31]** The theme of the Galilean witnesses is a major one in the Gospel of Luke and in Acts and is used to signify the continuity between the teachings of Jesus and the teachings of the church and to guarantee the fidelity of the church's teachings to the words of Jesus.
* **[38–39] Justified:** the verb is the same as that used in Paul's letters to speak of the experience of justification and, as in Paul, is here connected with the term "to have faith" ("every believer"). But this seems the only passage about Paul in Acts where justification is mentioned. In Lucan fashion it is paralleled with "forgiveness of sins" (a theme at Acts 2:38; 3:19; 5:31; 10:43) based on Jesus' resurrection (Acts 13:37) rather than his cross, and is put negatively (Acts 13:38). Therefore, some would translate, "in regard to everything from which you could not be acquitted ... every believer is acquitted."
* **[46]** The refusal to believe frustrates God's plan for his chosen people; however, no adverse judgment is made here concerning their ultimate destiny. Again, Luke, in the words of Paul, speaks of the priority of Israel in the plan for salvation (see Acts 10:36).
* **[51]** See note on Lk 9:5.

CHAPTER 14

* **14[8–18]** In an effort to convince his hearers that the divine power works through his word, Paul cures the cripple. However, the pagan tradition of the occasional appearance of

gods among human beings leads the people astray in interpreting the miracle. The incident reveals the cultural difficulties with which the church had to cope. Note the similarity of the miracle worked here by Paul to the one performed by Peter in Acts 3:2–10.

* **[12] Zeus ... Hermes**: in Greek religion, Zeus was the chief of the Olympian gods, the "father of gods and men"; Hermes was a son of Zeus and was usually identified as the herald and messenger of the gods.

* **[14] Tore their garments**: a gesture of protest.

* **[15–17]** This is the first speech of Paul to Gentiles recorded by Luke in Acts (cf. Acts 17:22–31). Rather than showing how Christianity is the logical outgrowth of Judaism, as he does in speeches before Jews, Luke says that God excuses past Gentile ignorance and then presents a natural theology arguing for the recognition of God's existence and presence through his activity in natural phenomena.

* **[23] They appointed presbyters**: the communities are given their own religious leaders by the traveling missionaries. The structure in these churches is patterned on the model of the Jerusalem community (Acts 11:30; 15:2, 5, 22; 21:18).

CHAPTER 15

* **15[1–35]** The Jerusalem "Council" marks the official rejection of the rigid view that Gentile converts were obliged to observe the Mosaic law completely. From here to the end of Acts, Paul and the Gentile mission become the focus of Luke's writing.

* **[1–5]** When some of the converted Pharisees of Jerusalem discover the results of the first missionary journey of Paul, they urge that the Gentiles be taught to follow the Mosaic law. Recognizing the authority of the Jerusalem church, Paul and Barnabas go there to settle the question of whether Gentiles can embrace a form of Christianity that does not include this obligation.

* **[6–12]** The gathering is possibly the same as that recalled by Paul in Gal 2:1–10. Note that in Acts 15:2 it is only the apostles and presbyters, a small group, with whom Paul and Barnabas are to meet. Here Luke gives the meeting a public character because he wishes to emphasize its doctrinal significance (see Acts 15:22).

* **[7–11]** Paul's refusal to impose the Mosaic law on the Gentile Christians is supported by Peter on the ground that within his own experience God bestowed the holy Spirit upon Cornelius and his household without preconditions concerning the adoption of the Mosaic law (see Acts 10:44–47).

* **[11]** In support of Paul, Peter formulates the fundamental meaning of the gospel: that all are invited to be saved through faith in the power of Christ.

* **[13–35]** Some scholars think that this apostolic decree suggested by James, the immediate leader of the Jerusalem community, derives from another historical occasion than the meeting in question. This seems to be the case if the meeting is the same as the one related in Gal 2:1–10. According to that account, nothing was imposed upon Gentile Christians in respect to Mosaic law; whereas the decree instructs Gentile Christians of mixed communities to abstain from meats sacrificed to idols and from blood-meats, and to avoid marriage within forbidden degrees of consanguinity and affinity (Lv 18), all of which practices were especially abhorrent to Jews. Luke seems to have telescoped two originally independent incidents here: the first a Jerusalem "Council" that dealt with the question of circumcision, and the second a Jerusalem decree dealing mainly with Gentile observance of dietary laws (see Acts 21:25 where Paul seems to be learning of the decree for the first time).

* **[14] Symeon**: elsewhere in Acts he is called either Peter or Simon. The presence of the name Symeon here suggests that, in the source Luke is using for this part of the Jerusalem "Council" incident, the name may have originally referred to

someone other than Peter (see Acts 13:1 where the Antiochene Symeon Niger is mentioned). As the text now stands, however, it is undoubtedly a reference to Simon Peter (Acts 15:7).

* **[34]** Some manuscripts add, in various wordings, "But Silas decided to remain there."

* **15[36]—18[22]** This continuous narrative recounts Paul's second missionary journey. On the internal evidence of the Lucan account, it lasted about three years. Paul first visited the communities he had established on his first journey (Acts 16:1–5), then pushed on into Macedonia, where he established communities at Philippi, Thessalonica, and Beroea (Acts 16:7—17:5). To escape the hostility of the Jews of Thessalonica, he left for Greece and while resident in Athens attempted, without success, to establish an effective Christian community there. From Athens he proceeded to Corinth and, after a stay of a year and a half, returned to Antioch by way of Ephesus and Jerusalem (Acts 17:16—18:22). Luke does not concern himself with the structure or statistics of the communities but aims to show the general progress of the gospel in the Gentile world as well as its continued failure to take root in the Jewish community.

CHAPTER 16

* **16[3] Paul had him circumcised**: he did this in order that Timothy might be able to associate with the Jews and so perform a ministry among them. Paul did not object to the Jewish Christians' adherence to the law. But he insisted that the law could not be imposed on the Gentiles. Paul himself lived in accordance with the law, or as exempt from the law, according to particular circumstances (see 1Cor 9:19–23).

* **[7] The Spirit of Jesus**: this is an unusual formulation in Luke's writings. The parallelism with Acts 16:6 indicates its meaning, the holy Spirit.

* **[10–17]** This is the first of the so-called "we-sections" in Acts, where Luke writes as one of Paul's companions. The other passages are Acts 20:5–15; 21:1–18; 27:1—28:16. Scholars debate whether Luke may not have used the first person plural simply as a literary device to lend color to the narrative. The realism of the narrative, however, lends weight to the argument that the "we" includes Luke or another companion of Paul whose data Luke used as a source.

* **[11–40]** The church at Philippi became a flourishing community to which Paul addressed one of his letters (see Introduction to the Letter to the Philippians).

* **[14] A worshiper of God**: a "God-fearer." See note on Acts 8:26–40.

* **[16] With an oracular spirit**: literally, "with a Python spirit." The Python was the serpent or dragon that guarded the Delphic oracle. It later came to designate a "spirit that pronounced oracles" and also a ventriloquist who, it was thought, had such a spirit in the belly.

* **[20] Magistrates**: in Greek, *stratēgoi*, the popular designation of the *duoviri*, the highest officials of the Roman colony of Philippi.

* **[35] The lictors**: the equivalent of police officers, among whose duties were the apprehension and punishment of criminals.

* **[37]** Paul's Roman citizenship granted him special privileges in regard to criminal process. Roman law forbade under severe penalty the beating of Roman citizens (see also Acts 22:25).

CHAPTER 17

* **17[6–7]** The accusations against Paul and his companions echo the charges brought against Jesus in Lk 23:2.

* **[7] There is another king, Jesus**: a distortion into a political sense of the apostolic proclamation of Jesus and the kingdom of God (see Acts 8:12).

* **[16–21]** Paul's presence in Athens sets the stage for the great

discourse before a Gentile audience in Acts 17:22–31. Although Athens was a politically insignificant city at this period, it still lived on the glories of its past and represented the center of Greek culture. The setting describes the conflict between Christian preaching and Hellenistic philosophy.

* [18] **Epicurean and Stoic philosophers**: for the followers of Epicurus (342–271 B.C.), the goal of life was happiness attained through sober reasoning and the searching out of motives for all choice and avoidance. The Stoics were followers of Zeno, a younger contemporary of Alexander the Great. Zeno and his followers believed in a type of pantheism that held that the spark of divinity was present in all reality and that, in order to be free, each person must live "according to nature." **This scavenger**: literally, "seed-picker," as of a bird that picks up grain. The word is later used of scrap collectors and of people who take other people's ideas and propagate them as if they were their own. **Promoter of foreign deities**: according to Xenophon, Socrates was accused of promoting new deities. The accusation against Paul echoes the charge against Socrates. **'Jesus' and 'Resurrection'**: the Athenians are presented as misunderstanding Paul from the outset; they think he is preaching about Jesus and a goddess named *Anastasis*, i.e., Resurrection.

* [19] **To the Areopagus**: the "Areopagus" refers either to the Hill of Ares west of the Acropolis or to the Council of Athens, which at one time met on the hill but which at this time assembled in the Royal Colonnade (*Stoa Basileios*).

* [22–31] In Paul's appearance at the Areopagus he preaches his climactic speech to Gentiles in the cultural center of the ancient world. The speech is more theological than christological. Paul's discourse appeals to the Greek world's belief in divinity as responsible for the origin and existence of the universe. It contests the common belief in a multiplicity of gods supposedly exerting their powers through their images. It acknowledges that the attempt to find God is a constant human endeavor. It declares, further, that God is the judge of the human race, that the time of the judgment has been determined, and that it will be executed through a man whom God raised from the dead. The speech reflects sympathy with pagan religiosity, handles the subject of idol worship gently, and appeals for a new examination of divinity, not from the standpoint of creation but from the standpoint of judgment.

* [23] **'To an Unknown God'**: ancient authors such as Pausanias, Philostratus, and Tertullian speak of Athenian altars with no specific dedication as altars of "unknown gods" or "nameless altars."

* [26] **From one**: many manuscripts read "from one blood." **Fixed ... seasons**: or "fixed limits to the epochs."

* [28] **'In him we live and move and have our being'**: some scholars understand this saying to be based on an earlier saying of Epimenides of Knossos (6th century B.C.). **'For we too are his offspring'**: here Paul is quoting Aratus of Soli, a third-century B.C. poet from Cilicia.

CHAPTER 18

* 18[2] **Aquila . . . Priscilla**: both may already have been Christians at the time of their arrival in Corinth (see Acts 18:26). According to 1Cor 16:19, their home became a meeting place for Christians. Claudius: the Emperor Claudius expelled the Jews from Rome ca. A.D. 49. The Roman historian Suetonius gives as reason for the expulsion disturbances among the Jews "at the instigation of Chrestos," probably meaning disputes about the messiahship of Jesus.

* [6] **Shook out his garments**: a gesture indicating Paul's repudiation of his mission to the Jews there; cf. Acts 28:17–31.

* [7] **A worshiper of God**: see note on Acts 8:26–40.

* [8] **Crispus**: in 1Cor 1:14 Paul mentions that Crispus was one of the few he himself baptized at Corinth.

* [12] **When Gallio was proconsul of Achaia**: Gallio's proconsulship in Achaia is dated to A.D. 51–52 from an inscription

discovered at Delphi. This has become an important date in establishing a chronology of the life and missionary work of Paul.

* [13] **Contrary to the law**: Gallio (Acts 18:15) understands this to be a problem of Jewish, not Roman, law.

* [18] **He had his hair cut because he had taken a vow**: a reference to a Nazirite vow (see Nm 6:1–21, especially, 6:18) taken by Paul (see also Acts 21:23–27).

* [22] **He went up and greeted the church**: "going up" suggests a visit to the church in Jerusalem.

* 18[23]—21[16] Luke's account of Paul's third missionary journey devotes itself mainly to his work at Ephesus (Acts 19:1—20:1). There is a certain restiveness on Paul's part and a growing conviction that the Spirit bids him return to Jerusalem and prepare to go to Rome (Acts 19:21).

* [24, 25] Apollos appears as a preacher who knows the teaching of Jesus in the context of John's baptism of repentance. Aquila and Priscilla instruct him more fully. He is referred to in 1Cor 1:12; 3:5–6, 22.

* [26] **The Way [of God]**: for the Way, see note on Acts 9:2. Other manuscripts here read "the Way of the Lord," "the word of the Lord," or simply "the Way."

CHAPTER 19

* 19[1–6] Upon his arrival in Ephesus, Paul discovers other people at the same religious stage as Apollos, though they seem to have considered themselves followers of Christ, not of the Baptist. On the relation between baptism and the reception of the Spirit, see note on Acts 8:16.

* [24] **Miniature silver shrines of Artemis**: the temple of Artemis at Ephesus was one of the seven wonders of the ancient world. Artemis, originally the Olympian virgin hunter, moon goddess, and goddess of wild nature, was worshiped at Ephesus as an Asian mother goddess and goddess of fertility. She was one of the most widely worshiped female deities in the Hellenistic world (see Acts 18:27).

* [31] **Asiarchs**: the precise status and role of the Asiarchs is disputed. They appear to have been people of wealth and influence who promoted the Roman imperial cult and who may also have been political representatives in a league of cities in the Roman province of Asia.

* [35] **Guardian of the temple**: this title was accorded by Rome to cities that provided a temple for the imperial cult. Inscriptional evidence indicates that Ephesus was acknowledged as the temple keeper of Artemis and of the imperial cult. **That fell from the sky**: many scholars think that this refers to a meteorite that was worshiped as an image of the goddess.

* [40] Some manuscripts omit the negative in **[not] be able**, making the meaning, "There is no cause for which we shall be able to give a reason for this demonstration."

CHAPTER 20

* 20[5] The second "we-section" of Acts begins here. See note on Acts 16:10–17.

* [6] **Feast of Unleavened Bread**: see note on Lk 22:1.

* [7] **The first day of the week**: the day after the sabbath and the first day of the Jewish week, apparently chosen originally by the Jerusalem community for the celebration of the liturgy of the Eucharist in order to relate it to the resurrection of Christ.

* [10] The action of Paul in throwing himself upon the dead boy recalls that of Elijah in 1Kgs 17:21 where the son of the widow of Zarephath is revived and that of Elisha in 2Kgs 4:34 where the Shunamite woman's son is restored to life.

* [16–35] Apparently aware of difficulties at Ephesus and neighboring areas, Paul calls the presbyters together at Miletus, about thirty miles from Ephesus. He reminds them of his dedication to the gospel (Acts 20:18–21), speaks of what he is about to suffer for the gospel (Acts 20:22–27), and admon-

ishes them to guard the community against false prophets, sure to arise upon his departure (Acts 20:28–31). He concludes by citing a saying of Jesus (Acts 20:35) not recorded in the gospel tradition. Luke presents this farewell to the Ephesian presbyters as Paul's last will and testament.

* [28] **Overseers**: see note on Phil 1:1. **The church of God**: because the clause "that he acquired with his own blood" following "the church of God" suggests that "his own blood" refers to God's blood, some early copyists changed "the church of God" to "the church of the Lord." Some prefer the translation "acquired with the blood of his own," i.e., Christ.

CHAPTER 21

* 21[1–18] The third "we-section" of Acts (see note on Acts 16:10–17).
* [8] **One of the Seven**: see note on Acts 6:2–4.
* [10] **Agabus**: mentioned in Acts 11:28 as the prophet who predicted the famine that occurred when Claudius was emperor.
* [11] The symbolic act of Agabus recalls those of Old Testament prophets. Compare Is 20:2; Ez 4:1; Jer 13:1.
* [14] The Christian disciples' attitude reflects that of Jesus (see Lk 22:42).
* [17–26] The leaders of the Jewish Christians of Jerusalem inform Paul that the Jews there believe he has encouraged the Jews of the diaspora to abandon the Mosaic law. According to Acts, Paul had no objection to the retention of the law by the Jewish Christians of Jerusalem and left the Jews of the diaspora who accepted Christianity free to follow the same practice.
* [23–26] The leaders of the community suggest that Paul, on behalf of four members of the Jerusalem community, make the customary payment for the sacrifices offered at the termination of the Nazirite vow (see Nm 6:1–24) in order to impress favorably the Jewish Christians in Jerusalem with his high regard for the Mosaic law. Since Paul himself had once made this vow (Acts 18:18), his respect for the law would be on public record.
* [24] **Pay their expenses**: according to Nm 6:14–15 the Nazirite had to present a yearling lamb for a holocaust, a yearling ewe lamb for a sin offering, and a ram for a peace offering, along with food and drink offerings, upon completion of the period of the vow.
* [25] Paul is informed about the apostolic decree, seemingly for the first time (see note on Acts 15:13–35). The allusion to the decree was probably introduced here by Luke to remind his readers that the Gentile Christians themselves were asked to respect certain Jewish practices deriving from the law.
* [28] The charges against Paul by the diaspora Jews are identical to the charges brought against Stephen by diaspora Jews in Acts 6:13. **Brought Greeks into the temple**: non-Jews were forbidden, under penalty of death, to go beyond the Court of the Gentiles. Inscriptions in Greek and Latin on a stone balustrade marked off the prohibited area.
* [31] **Cohort commander**: literally, "the leader of a thousand in a cohort." At this period the Roman cohort commander usually led six hundred soldiers, a tenth of a legion; but the number in a cohort varied.
* [36] **Away with him**: at the trial of Jesus before Pilate in Lk 23:18, the people similarly shout, "Away with this man."
* [38] **The Egyptian**: according to the Jewish historian Josephus, an Egyptian gathered a large crowd on the Mount of Olives to witness the destruction of the walls of Jerusalem that would fall at the Egyptian "prophet's" word. The commotion was put down by the Roman authorities and the Egyptian escaped, but only after thousands had been killed. **Four thousand assassins**: literally, *sicarii*. According to Josephus, these were political nationalists who removed their opponents by assassination with a short dagger, called in Latin a *sica*.
* [40] **In Hebrew**: meaning, perhaps, in Aramaic, which at this time was the Semitic tongue in common use.

CHAPTER 22

* 22[1–21] Paul's first defense speech is presented to the Jerusalem crowds. Luke here presents Paul as a devout Jew (Acts 22:3) and zealous persecutor of the Christian community (Acts 22:4–5), and then recounts the conversion of Paul for the second time in Acts (see note on Acts 9:1–19).
* [15] **His witness**: like the Galilean followers during the historical ministry of Jesus, Paul too, through his experience of the risen Christ, is to be a witness to the resurrection (compare Acts 1:8; 10:39–41; Lk 24:48).
* [21] Paul endeavors to explain that his position on the law has not been identical with that of his audience because it has been his prophetic mission to preach to the Gentiles to whom the law was not addressed and who had no faith in it as a way of salvation.
* [22] Paul's suggestion that his prophetic mission to the Gentiles did not involve his imposing the law on them provokes the same opposition as occurred in Pisidian Antioch (Acts 13:45).
* [25] **Is it lawful for you to scourge a man who is a Roman citizen and has not been tried?**: see note on Acts 16:37.

CHAPTER 23

* 23[2] **The high priest Ananias**: Ananias, son of Nedebaeus, was high priest from A.D. 47 to 59.
* [3] **God will strike you**: Josephus reports that Ananias was later assassinated in A.D. 66 at the beginning of the First Revolt.
* [5] Luke portrays Paul as a model of one who is obedient to the Mosaic law. Paul, because of his reverence for the law (Ex 22:27), withdraws his accusation of hypocrisy, "whitewashed wall" (cf. Mt 23:27), when he is told Ananias is the high priest.
* [11] The occurrence of the vision of Christ consoling Paul and assuring him that he will be his witness in Rome prepares the reader for the final section of Acts: the journey of Paul and the word he preaches to Rome under the protection of the Romans.
* [17] **Centurions**: a centurion was a military officer in charge of one hundred soldiers.
* [23] **By nine o'clock tonight**: literally, "by the third hour of the night." The night hours began at 6 P.M. **Two hundred auxiliaries**: the meaning of the Greek is not certain. It seems to refer to spearmen from the local police force and not from the cohort of soldiers, which would have numbered only 500–1000 men.
* [26–30] The letter emphasizes the fact that Paul is a Roman citizen and asserts the lack of evidence that he is guilty of a crime against the empire. The tone of the letter implies that the commander became initially involved in Paul's case because of his Roman citizenship, but this is not an exact description of what really happened (see Acts 21:31–33; 22:25–29).
* [26] M. Antonius Felix was procurator of Judea from A.D. 52 to 60. His procuratorship was marked by cruelty toward and oppression of his Jewish subjects.

CHAPTER 24

* 24[5] **Nazoreans**: that is, followers of Jesus of Nazareth.
* [7] The Western text has added here a verse (really 6b–8a) that is not found in the best Greek manuscripts. It reads, "and would have judged him according to our own law, but the cohort commander Lysias came and violently took him out of our hands and ordered his accusers to come before you."
* [10–21] Whereas the advocate Tertullus referred to Paul's activities on his missionary journeys, the apostle narrowed the charges down to the riot connected with the incident in the temple (see Acts 21:27–30; 24:17–20). In his defense, Paul stresses the continuity between Christianity and Judaism.
* [24, 25] The way of Christian discipleship greatly disquiets Fe-

lix, who has entered into an adulterous marriage with Drusilla, daughter of Herod Agrippa I. This marriage provides the background for the topics Paul speaks about and about which Felix does not want to hear.

[27] Very little is known of Porcius Festus who was a procurator of Judea from A.D. 60 to 62.

HAPTER 25

25[2] Even after two years the animosity toward Paul in Jerusalem had not subsided (see Acts 24:27).

[9–12] Paul refuses to acknowledge that the Sanhedrin in Jerusalem has any jurisdiction over him now (Acts 25:11). Paul uses his right as a Roman citizen to appeal his case to the jurisdiction of the Emperor (Nero, ca. A.D. 60) (Acts 25:12). This move broke the deadlock between Roman protective custody of Paul and the plan of his enemies to kill him (25:3).

[13] **King Agrippa and Bernice**: brother and sister, children of Herod Agrippa I whose activities against the Jerusalem community are mentioned in Acts 12:1–19. Agrippa II was a petty ruler over small areas in northern Palestine and some villages in Perea. His influence on the Jewish population of Palestine was insignificant.

HAPTER 26

26[2–23] Paul's final defense speech in Acts is now made before a king (see Acts 9:15). In the speech Paul presents himself as a zealous Pharisee and Christianity as the logical development of Pharisaic Judaism. The story of his conversion is recounted for the third time in Acts in this speech (see note on Acts 9:1–19).

[4] **Among my people**: that is, among the Jews.

[14] **In Hebrew**: see note on Acts 21:40. **It is hard for you to kick against the goad**: this proverb is commonly found in Greek literature and in this context signifies the senselessness and ineffectiveness of any opposition to the divine influence in his life.

[16] The words of Jesus directed to Paul here reflect the dialogues between Christ and Ananias (Acts 9:15) and between Ananias and Paul (Acts 22:14–15) in the two previous accounts of Paul's conversion.

[18] **To open their eyes**: though no mention is made of Paul's blindness in this account (cf. Acts 9:8–9, 12, 18; 22:11–13), the task he is commissioned to perform is the removal of other people's spiritual blindness.

[22] **Saying nothing different from what the prophets and Moses foretold**: see note on Lk 18:31.

[23] **That the Messiah must suffer**: see note on Lk 24:26.

[26] **Not done in a corner**: for Luke, this Greek proverb expresses his belief that he is presenting a story about Jesus and the church that is already well known. As such, the entire history of Christianity is public knowledge and incontestable. Luke presents his story in this way to provide "certainty" to his readers about the instructions they have received (Lk 1:4).

[27, 28] If the Christian missionaries proclaim nothing different from what the Old Testament prophets had proclaimed (Acts 26:22–23), then the logical outcome for the believing Jew, according to Luke, is to become a Christian.

[31–32] In recording the episode of Paul's appearance before Agrippa, Luke wishes to show that, when Paul's case was judged impartially, no grounds for legal action against him were found (see Acts 23:29; 25:25).

CHAPTER 27

* 27[1]—28[16] Here Luke has written a stirring account of adventure on the high seas, incidental to his main purpose of showing how well Paul got along with his captors and how his prophetic influence saved the lives of all on board. The recital also establishes the existence of Christian communities in Puteoli and Rome. This account of the voyage and shipwreck also constitutes the final "we-section" in Acts (see note on Acts 16:10–17).

* [1] **Cohort Augusta**: the presence of a Cohort Augusta in Syria during the first century A.D. is attested in inscriptions. Whatever the historical background to this information given by Luke may be, the name Augusta serves to increase the prominence and prestige of the prisoner Paul whose custodians bear so important a Roman name.

* [9] **The time of the fast**: the fast kept on the occasion of the Day of Atonement (Lv 16:29–31), which occurred in late September or early October.

* [35] **He took bread . . .**: the words recall the traditional language of the celebration of the Eucharist (see Lk 22:19).

CHAPTER 28

* 28[4] **Justice**: in Greek mythology, the pursuing goddess of vengeance and justice.

* [11] **Dioscuri**: that is, the Twin Brothers, Castor and Pollux, the sons of Zeus and the patrons of the sailors.

* [16] With Paul's arrival in Rome, the programmatic spread of the word of the Lord to "the ends of the earth" (Acts 1:8) is accomplished. In Rome, Paul is placed under house arrest, and under this mild form of custody he is allowed to proclaim the word in the capital of the civilized world of his day.

* [17–22] Paul's first act in Rome is to learn from the leaders of the Jewish community whether the Jews of Jerusalem plan to pursue their case against him before the Roman jurisdiction. He is informed that no such plan is afoot, but that the Jews of Rome have heard the Christian teaching denounced. Paul's offer to explain it to them is readily accepted.

* [20] **The hope of Israel**: in the words of Paul (Acts 23:6), Luke has identified this hope as hope in the resurrection of the dead.

* [25–28] Paul's final words in Acts reflect a major concern of Luke's writings: how the salvation promised in the Old Testament, accomplished by Jesus, and offered first to Israel (Acts 13:26), has now been offered to and accepted by the Gentiles. Quoting Is 6:9–10, Paul presents the scriptural support for his indictment of his fellow Jews who refuse to accept the message he proclaims. Their rejection leads to its proclamation among the Gentiles.

* [29] The Western text has added here a verse that is not found in the best Greek manuscripts: "And when he had said this, the Jews left, seriously arguing among themselves."

* [30–31] Although the ending of Acts may seem to be abrupt, Luke has now completed his story with the establishment of Paul and the proclamation of Christianity in Rome. Paul's confident and unhindered proclamation of the gospel in Rome forms the climax to the story whose outline was provided in Acts 1:8—"You will be my witnesses in Jerusalem ... and to the ends of the earth."

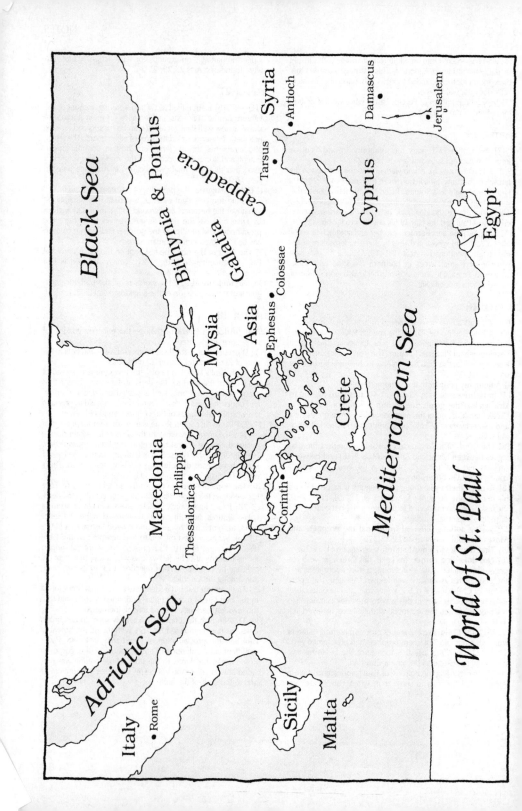

World of St. Paul

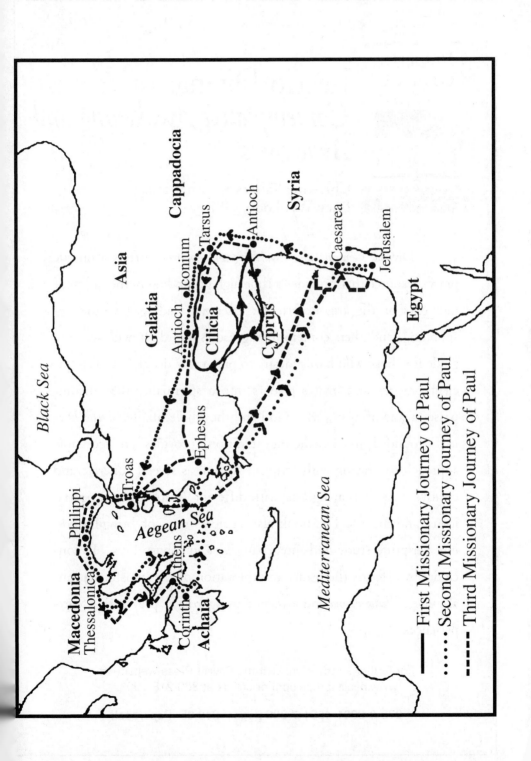

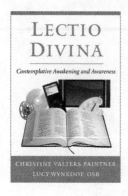

Lectio Divina:
Contemplative Awakening and Awareness

Christine Valters Paintner and Lucy Wynkoop, OSB

Lectio Divina: *Contemplative Awakening and Awareness* offers a unique prayer resource that provides a thorough grounding in the different moments of the *lectio* experience: listening, reading, savoring, responding, and then contemplating God's Word. It will act as a guide for those who have a desire to pray more deeply into this ancient practice and invites readers into a spirituality that encompasses a way of being with God and the whole of life. *Lectio Divina*, grounded in Benedictine tradition, provides an accessible approach to praying with scripture as well as several concrete and creative ways of praying *lectio* with different "texts" such as poetry, icons, and movies. The book also explores ways of bringing *lectio* into scripture study and integrating *lectio* into busy lives. It concludes by offering the reader an exploration of the transformational value of *lectio divina* and a way of using *lectio* to pray with life experience.

For further information, visit the Paulist Press website at
www.paulistpress.com or call us at 800-218-1903.

978-0-8091-4531-7 208 pages $18.95 Paperback